# Navigating Transitions

# 风雨同舟

——自闭症,你的人生过客

【美】MICHELLE LIU 著

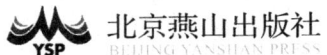

图书在版编目（CIP）数据

风雨同舟 / Michelle Liu 著．—北京：北京燕山出版社，2017.9

ISBN 978-7-5402-4674-7

Ⅰ．①风… Ⅱ．①M… Ⅲ．①缄默症－儿童教育－特殊教育 Ⅳ．① G766

中国版本图书馆 CIP 数据核字（2017）第 227119 号

## 风雨同舟

| | |
|---|---|
| 作　　者 | Michelle Liu |
| 责任编辑 | 金贝伦　王　迪 |
| 设　　计 | 展　华 |
| 责任校对 | 张瑞武 |
| 地　　址 | 北京市西城区陶然亭路 53 号 |
| 电　　话 | 010-65240430 |
| 邮　　编 | 100054 |
| 印　　刷 | 廊坊市博林印务有限公司 |
| 开　　本 | 889mm×1194mm　1/32 |
| 字　　数 | 60 千字 |
| 印　　张 | 8.625 |
| 版　　次 | 2017 年 9 月第 1 版 |
| 印　　次 | 2017 年 9 月第 1 次印刷 |
| 定　　价 | 32.00 元 |
| 出版发行 | 北京燕山出版社　BEIJING YANSHAN PRESS |

版权所有　盗版必究

# Preface

Michelle Liu is a talented writer and passionate young woman. Her idea to write this book stems from her compassionate nature to help others. After she introduced the idea of a student run club to help people and families affected by autism, Michelle began to learn as much as she could about autism and the impact on families affected by autism. Her relentless pursuit of knowledge and her genuine personality allowed her to meet families and learn their stories. After many hours of research, Michelle has collected the narratives of these families in this work to share with others.

Dennis J. Lepold
Principal
West Windsor-Plainsboro High School South

## Self-Introduction

Transitions can be hard for everyone. Whether it is moving to a new school or home, or becoming an adult, such changes interrupt everyday routine. Those of us who have had to adjust have learned the importance of planning ahead.

For parents with children on the autism spectrum, such planning takes years and requires extensive research. Preparation must start after the initial diagnosis.

At Rutgers Medical School, I worked with Dr. Walter Zahorodny to review the reports of hundreds of children ( aged 2-8 ) with autism. In these cases, parents expressed elevated concerns about their child's behavior- impulsivity, delayed communication, and troubles with sleeping and eating. I was struck by their perseverance. Although there are manuals available to them through doctors or websites, I wanted to provide a personal resource in which families could draw directly from similar experiences of others. A small success is sometimes the result of months, or years of determination and to reach a milestone is an unforgettable moment. As children on the spectrum become adults, even more goals are set. It is a difficult time, but with proper support and guidance, the likelihood of independence, and being able to handle responsibilities is increased. In a society that "may be inadequate to accommodate the needs of youths with ASD" (National Institute of Health), preparing for different transition stages is essential. I hope my book will highlight the important steps parents and individuals with autism should take when navigating this journey.

This book would not have been possible without the tremendous support of my mother, Jian, Dr. Zahorodny, and my advisor Dr. Jim Ball. For the last three years, Dr. Ball, co-chairperson of the Autism Society of America, has welcomed my questions about autism. He generously shared his expertise in the field and encouraged my involvement in research. In addition, I thank everyone who I spoke with- their willingness to share their stories testify their kindness. I thank Scholastic Art and Writing Awards for recognizing my work and to my past English teachers- Ms. Hutchinson and Ms. Glassband- who fostered my passion for writing. Finally, I thank each and every one of the children I have worked with. They have taught me how labels such as autism do not limit our beliefs or experiences. While it may be hard, choosing to embrace these differences makes each step forward all the more courageous.

# Editor's Introduction

Most Chinese people are unfamiliar with autism, a serious neurological and developmental disorder. When trying to help a child on the autism spectrum they feel unprepared and overwhelmed. There are millions of autism patient in China. Survey shows parents of autism children have qualms about the future, stressing over whether their child may achieve independence when they reach adulthood. How to complete a smooth transition from adolescence to adulthood is an important step in integrating individuals with autism into society.

Compared to developed Western countries, China is in its initial stages of autism acknowledgement, treatment, recovery, education, employment and social security. In the United States, education professionals and scientists have been researching the best methods for autism intervention and therapy since the 1940s. The results of their studies prompted governments and institutes to establish an intricate system which offers comprehensive support to individuals on the spectrum, such as early intervention, enrolling autism children in public elementary and middle school, then vocational school, even for college.

The young author of this book, Michelle Liu, is a Chinese-American. For a long time, she has worked and volunteered with autistic youth. Not only has she helped build their confidence, but she has also coached them to embrace life with positivity. Michelle not only is the founder of Ambassadors for Autism at her high school, but she also is involved with several New Jersey autism advocacy groups. From raising over a thousand dollars to support autism research to organizing a summer camp for autistic children, she is an active member in the community. During this period, as Michelle interacted with families impacted by autism, she collected information about their individual cases. In this book, she has selected seven representative stories. Her work provides precious information to parents and interested people who hope to understand autism.

Autism is no long to be scared of, and no one should feel unprepared or overwhelmed. With more attention and love from society, children with autism will better be able to transition to adulthood.

对于大多数中国人而言，自闭症是遥远和陌生的。当它近在咫尺时，又是深感恐惧和无助。在中国，患自闭症的人口可能数以百万计。调查显示，多数患者的家长对孩子未来成人后有独立生活的能力缺乏信心。如何顺利完成从少年到成人的过渡是帮助自闭症患者回归社会的重要一步。

与西方发达国家相比，中国对自闭症患者的认知，治疗，康复、教育、就业、安置和社会保障等几个重要环节中还处于刚刚开始的阶段。以美国为例，从20世纪40年代教育和心理学专家、学者对这一病症积极探索其病因、治疗手段、干预方法等，累计了大量的研究成果。政府和社会机构相应建立了一套完整的体系：从患儿被诊断、接受早期干预、融入主流小学、中学，进入职业教育或者大学，一路的成长过程中都提供了一条龙服务，为自闭症患者最终独立生活提供有效的帮助。

本书的小作者Michelle Liu，是一位出生在美国的华裔女孩。

长期以来，她一直关注和热心参与辅导社区自闭症青少年，帮助他们建立信心，乐观的去面对生活。她不仅在所在高中成立自闭症学生帮助组织，更是多个美国新泽西州自闭症组织的活跃分子，从参与为自闭症患者募捐的马拉松到策划组织为自闭症儿童开办夏令营。Michelle在和自闭症孩子及家属互动过程中，她积累了大量个案信息。在采访多位自闭症患者和家属后，作者在本书中记录了七位具有代表性的自闭症少年到成年过渡的过程。给有兴趣关注了解自闭症的父母及相关人士提供了值得参考的宝贵经验。自闭症并不可怕，家长们也不再无助和焦虑。越来越多来自社会的温情和关注如何在帮助自闭症青少年顺利过渡到成年期。

编辑组

# Contents 目录

**J**ames ....................................... 1
詹姆斯 ..................................... 14

**E**mily ....................................... 24
艾米莉 ..................................... 37

**D**ylan ....................................... 47
迪伦 ....................................... 58

**M**att ........................................ 66
马特 ....................................... 81

**A**shley ..................................... 92
阿什莉 ................................... 106

**D**avid ..................................... 117
大卫 ..................................... 125

**P**eter ..................................... 131
皮特 ..................................... 142

**F**urther Reading ............... 151
附录 ..................................... 151

# James

James is a 33-year old with Asperger's-he's juggling a job at Shoprite, a relationship with his boyfriend Mark, and a potential singing career. James is also eloquent-his vocabulary is tantamount to an English professor's-and fluid with his words. But as a disabled dependent, a victim of PTSD, social anxiety, and depression, James's life was not always happy-go-lucky. In fact, most of it, he says, has been plagued by suppression and abuse.

In 1982, James Albright was born as the son of two strictly-Catholic, Irish parents in Staten Island, New York. On the surface, he lived a modest lifestyle-his father was a stockbroker at Morgan Stanley, and his mother was the caretaker of James's two younger sisters and older half sister. Past this facade, James was suffering deeply.

Even "suffering" might be an understatement, however.

*Navigating Transitions*
风雨同舟

On the eve of his first birthday, James burnt himself when a pot fell from a kitchen cabinet, splattering hot coffee onto his skin. The incident scarred his left hand, right in the area between his thumb and third finger.

Although he doesn't recall the exact sensation he felt, James replays this traumatic moment over and over as an adult and recognizes the accident as a predecessor to his future pains. "I learned to live in abject fear and severe vulnerability," James says.

From a young age, despite being "very spoiled," James developed a rocky relationship with his parents and grew to despise their large trust fund. In fact, his father showed no understanding of his emotions, revering him as a paragon of virtue, providing his son a slew of toys and games.

"My family was toxic," James admits, "they thought I was some trophy they could revere. In a sense, I was dehumanized; everyone around me was wiping away the down parts that made me human. They would deny I had any flaws and they would spoil me regularly. They put me so high up that they couldn't even see who I was anymore. Once, my father spent a $1000 DJ kit for me when I was 12 and experiencing with mixtapes. In another case, on

James

our first family trip to Disney World, I wanted this foot-tall Eiffel tower from Epcot. So, since I pretty much inherited my father's narcissism, I sat there and refused to leave the store without it. I think my parents expected me to follow them after they left the store, but to my surprise, my father came back and said to me, 'I'll get you the tower.' I said, 'Are you sure? Do you really want to do this?' and he replied, 'I hate to refuse you.' He should have never [bought me the tower] in hindsight. And what upsets me is that my father never taught me the values of hard work; he just plopped everything right into my hands, hoping I would just cooperate with him and basically, agree with whatever he said. Spoilage."

James's father was also incredibly stubborn, adamant that his son takes on a "respectable position" similar to his own. James' father brought him to work, introducing his son to his office above Wall Street. To appease his parents' wills, James said "yes" to stockbroking. Consequently, he experienced Stockholm Syndrome, "the psychological response in which captives begin to identify their captors closely."

"They would make me feel guilt, shame, and fear as if I was doing something wrong whenever I disagreed with them on even

Navigating Transitions
风雨同舟

the most subjective topics. They would portray sex, for example, as evil." James claims.

His father, in particular, would blackmail him emotionally, convincing James that "he would do nothing to harm his son now, would he?" Essentially, if James's opinions deviated even slightly from his elders, he was reprimanded.

"In Catholicism, you are taught to be very, very obedient and to succumb to your parent's demands." James says, "But respect is a two-way street. So, for most of my youth, I was denied of my opinions. I was living in a nightmare, but at the same time, a fantasy world where I was sheltered-naive-and wasn't exposed to the real world. My entire family handled me like china, but they held onto me so tight, that I eventually shattered. Their treatment is also a huge part of why they dismissed so many of my struggles-especially with Aspergers-they thought I was perfect."

As a loquacious and socially active child, few adults suspected James possessed any form of autism, however. When he was a toddler, he attended a Montessori daycare and made many of his most precious memories at the school. But in elementary school, his disability surfaced.

James vividly recalls his confrontations with Mr. Paulson, a

James

narcissistic middle school teacher. "I've always had many specific interests throughout my childhood-that's a common autistic trait, we fixate on a specific subject and devote 110% of ourselves to learning about it and enjoying it. So, at the time, I was obsessed with the Superman logo. And I was spending most of the days in computer class drawing it on the computer. And at one point, Mr. Paulson said to me that he wanted me to try out something else. Well, I didn't feel like trying out something else, so I redid it. What did my teacher do? He banned me from the computers for a few minutes and told me to write down what I did wrong. And he said to me, 'I am very disappointed in you,' among other things. But how dare he force me to give up what I wanted at that moment and implore me to do something I did not want to do. In another incident, every week we would go swimming at the YMCA. One day, I did not feel like going swimming, and I tried to explain that to Mr. Paulson. And what did he do? He threatened to take away some of the classes I enjoyed, like computers and what not. That got me in the pool. He blackmailed me, just like my father. People realized I was too perfect for that school and they were jealous of me. So, I think much of the experience I had in the public academy was pretty traumatic."

Evidently, James's deteriorating mental stability was propelled by bullying as well. James recalls, "When I was a kid, beginning at 6, 7, or 8, I became obsessed with Madonna because she was, at the time, at the top of her game. And all my peers, I guess they learned it from their parents, they teased me for it. They thought she was terrible and I said 'stop that, she is not terrible.' One day, my third-grade teacher tried to teach me a lesson. She said, 'Do you like Bruce Springsteen, James?' and I said, 'No, not really.' and she responded, 'Well that hurts me because I have all his albums.' But I failed to convey to her, and she failed to understand I wasn't trying to disparage her, I was just trying to say,

'Hey, he's just not my cup of tea.' But the kids were going a step further and saying, 'Oh, she [Madonna] is bad, she's this, she's that, They were like demonizing her. And this made me feel really alone in the world."

Despite living in utter bliss, James's parents were curious to why their son seemed so offbeat. In 1996, James, a ripe teenager, was diagnosed with autism, specifically Asperger's-a mild form of autism-not yet categorized at the time. He was taken to a myriad of doctors, though his parents never told him why he was constantly barraged by questions about his mental health. "I was

very confused why we were always visiting doctor, after doctor," James remembers, "I thought, is there something wrong with me?"

In a seemingly caring effort to hide the truth from their son, James's parents didn't reveal to him that he had Asperger's for his entire childhood. Instead, he was sent to a speech therapist. From 1996 to 2000, the expert taught James to communicate with his peers. "The skills I needed to listen to them, to draw information out of them by asking them questions because, before that, I was narcissistically talking about myself. Again, a blur between my autism and my father's family trauma. But now, of course, I show interests in other people's feelings because it's the right thing to do. I learned empathy. Before, I didn't have real empathy. I have progressed, but I am always reminded of the journey of how broken I am."

Afterward, James was sent to a Wolfson Academy, a special needs school 15 minutes away from his home. Each classroom, he describes, had about 10 kids and everything was "made more fun than usual." At the school, James integrated with his peers and regained a sense of freedom that was robbed from his childhood.

At 18, on the threshold of independence, James was

complacent at Wolfson. A few years ago, he had tried to convince his father to help him pay for singing lessons, pitching that he wanted to emulate the works of Jackson, Houston, and of course, Madonna. His father had scoffed at the idea and instead suggested that his son attend a nearby university. "My father wanted for me to be an exact clone of him," James utters, "The problem was, I didn't want to go to university. At Wolfson, people could stay at the institution until they turned 21 and that is what I wanted to do. My parents, however, pushed me to go to college, 'Try it.' they said. And so, I had to go to university, and the whole experience was miserable. And you know what? When I dropped out two and a half years later, they said to me, 'Well maybe you should have stayed at Wolfson. At least you tried.' That time, I snapped like a tree branch under pressure, because my family never built for me a foundation. And when I was at this critical time in my life, I thought, how does my family expect me to do all this, after sheltering me, after burdening me with inappropriateness and mal-activity. Did they expect God to all of a sudden wave his hand? Cause that is certainly how my father acted."

Suddenly, at this critical point in his life, James's parents revealed to him the secret they had shrouded his entire youth:

James

his Asperger's diagnosis. James was in shock-he had always understood there was something different about him, but he had never realized the degree of his impairment. Coupled with the constant expectation to be perfect, James crippled under despair and shock. "At first, I was in denial. Then, I felt like the world owed me something," James says, "I had spent so many nights wondering why I was so different and when my parents told me it was because of my autism, I lashed out. It was the worst time in my life; I started acting as if I had a severe form of autism. I wanted to take back all my parents could have done for me when I was younger but kept hidden because they were in denial that their son wasn't perfect." Plagued by mood irregularities and PTSD, James made an attempt to end his life in 2003.

Despite being hospitalized and undergoing therapy as an outpatient ( culminating in 8 ECT treatments ) , James sank into depression the following year. Later, he would describe the agony as "only the tip of the iceberg" . Although James had come to terms with his Asperger's, members of his family still dismissed the diagnosis as fictitious. "I have a cousin; her name is Teresa, lives in Staten Island." James says, "she tried to reassure me on Facebook, in an emotionally blackmailing way, you don't have it.

You don't have it. And I said to her calmly, 'Teresa, I have the symptoms, I was diagnosed.'"

Ultimately, the first step of James's recovery was finding a job. "It was a long, long, rocky road to find employment. I had just finished a stint at a rehabilitation clinic and really limited myself regarding flexibility and availability, in fear of a mental breakdown. My job coaches really did help, though; together, we worked on my resume. First, I tried for a job at Newark Airport, serving food. But, since I lived too far away, they were hesitant to hire me, and I decided it wasn't the commute. I applied to my current job at Shoprite, and the employer loved my personality. I was hired as a seasonal worker, but eventually, I was let go, due to a messy financial situation. All the meantime, I was still in an emotional abyss. Plenty of my happy moods were fleeting and sad memories from my childhood were always lurking. Sometimes, I would have rough spots on the job, and I was unable to deal with certain customers who were very aggressive. Because of my poor social skills-I still felt impaired because of my Aspergers-I would sometimes engage in altercations with my coworkers or invade other people's personal space, without even knowing it. I felt as if I was riding on an emotional roller coaster and I was starting to

get nauseous."

Wanting to find a supportive partner, James started to open himself up to more strangers. In 2010, he met his boyfriend Mark, who James describes as "a godsend."

"Mark shined the light where it needed to be. He challenged how my family raised me and wasn't scared to share his opinions openly with my father. Of course, my family thought Mark was trying to take me away from them." With Mark's patient guidance, James was able to overcome "a lot of the autistic limitations, though it had come at a heavy price to his psyche".

Working full time at Shoprite again, James realizes how the past has molded the character he is today. "If my parents hadn't kept my disability a secret, I would have learned to accept my quirks. Now, however, I am forced to relive the horrors of my childhood, living with PTSD. Currently, I am still at home with my father. I am aided by the government because of my autism through Medicare and social security disability, but unfortunately, I had to come out as a disabled dependent to receive these financial benefits. When my father retired in 2010, I was able to accept more money as a disabled dependent under a retiree, but honestly, I just want to be in a house of my own. Although I don't

qualify for subsidized housing, I want to feel unencumbered, unburdened by the traumas of my past."

    Looking out the window, he tells the story of one of the greatest moments of his life, the time he met Glenn Scarpelli. Like himself, Glenn is Italian, gay and from Staten Island. In January, when James started watching One Day at a Time, he was captivated by Glenn's performance as Alex Handris in the 1980s show. On a whim, James now calls it, he messaged Glenn on Facebook. To his surprise, Glenn responded and told James that he would be at a local theater the next month for a meet and greet. In fact, Glenn coined a nickname for James: "His fellow gay Staten Islander." For the week leading up to the event, James acted up, unable to contain his excitement. "I didn't want Glenn to think I was a creepy stalker. So I was thinking to myself, how do I modify my behavior, so he doesn't believe that? Fortunately, on the day that I went there, my behavior was well enough and when I told him who I was-his fellow gay Staten Islander from Facebook-the way his face lit up, I would never forget that. He was so happy to see me, and one thing I had wished for is I would get to hug him, and I didn't get to have to worry about that because he jumped right out of his seat and hugged me. It was like two

James

friends. And at this time, Glenn had just turned 50, and I had never been infatuated with a 50-year-old. But there was something special about Glenn." James pulls out his phone and presents a picture that captured their meeting. On the left, Glenn dons a crisp blue shirt and James, a bright yellow T-shirt. James has slung his right arm around Glenn, and they are both beaming. "These moments," James says, "are what makes life special. It was so cathartic talking to Glenn, and in moments when I'm struggling with autism, or with my PTSD, I just remember the way Glenn's face glowed up. That I'll treasure forever."

# 詹姆斯

今年33岁的詹姆斯患有阿斯伯格综合征,目前他在绍普莱特工作,有男朋友马克,还有潜在的歌唱生涯。詹姆斯很雄辩,说话流利,他的词汇量相当于英语教授。但是作为残疾人,再加上受创伤后应激障碍综合征(Post-Traumatic Stress Disorder, PTSD)、社交恐惧症、抑郁症的影响,詹姆斯的生活不是很快乐。詹姆斯说,事实上这主要是因为一直饱受压制和虐待。

1982年,詹姆斯·奥尔布赖特出生于纽约州史坦顿岛的一个家庭,父母都是爱尔兰人,两人都是严格的天主教徒。表面上看,他的生活朴素和谐,父亲是摩根士丹利的股票经纪人,母亲照料着詹姆斯的两个妹妹和一个同母异父的姐姐。实际上,詹姆斯饱受痛苦。

然而,即使用"饱受痛苦"可能也不足以形容他的处境。

生日前夕,詹姆斯打落了橱柜里的一只锅,热咖啡洒到了皮肤上烫伤了自己。这次意外在他的左手大拇指和三指之间留

詹姆斯

下了疤痕。

虽然不记得当时确切的感觉了，成年的詹姆斯还是不断回想这个痛苦的时刻，意识到这场意外是未来痛苦的前身。"我学会了在极度恐惧和脆弱中生活。"詹姆斯说。

尽管从小备受"宠溺"，詹姆斯和父母的关系一直不太融洽，开始鄙视他们的大型信托基金。事实上，父亲不懂他的情绪，推崇他为完美的典范，给他一大堆玩具和游戏。

"我的家庭爱摆布人。"詹姆斯承认说，"他们把我当作可以推崇的战利品。在某种意义上，我的人性被剥夺，身边的每个人都在擦掉我身上不好的部分。他们否认我的缺点，经常宠我。总之，他们把我摆得太高，以至于都不认得我是谁了。我12岁时正在听混音专辑，父亲曾花了1000美元为我买了一套DJ设备。还有一次，在我们的第一次迪士尼世界家庭之旅中，我想要未来世界（Epcot）商店里一英尺高的埃菲尔铁塔，因为几乎遗传了父亲的自恋，所以我坐在那里，没有铁塔就不离开。我以为父母亲走出商店后会希望我能跟出来，但令我惊讶的是，父亲又走了回来并对我说：'我会买给你的。'我问道：'真的吗？你真的愿意买给我吗？'父亲回答：'当然！我不喜欢拒绝你。'现在看来，他不该给我买那个铁塔的。让我烦恼的是，父亲从来没教过我努力工作的价值，只是一味地把所有东西都递到我手上，希望我能配合他，基本上听话。教子无方！"

詹姆斯的父亲还非常顽固，固执地认为儿子有着和自己一样的"受人尊敬的地位"。父亲还带詹姆斯去上班，把他介绍给华尔街办公室的人。为了安抚父母的意志，詹姆斯姑且对股票经纪活动表示了"赞同"。结果，詹姆斯因此有了斯德哥尔摩综合征，这是"一种俘虏开始对捕捉者产生亲密情感的心理反应"。

"当我跟父母意见相左时，他们会让我感到内疚、耻辱和恐惧，就好像我做错了事情，即便是对于非常主观的话题也会如此。比如，他们会把性描述成邪恶的事物。"詹姆斯说。

特别是父亲会在情感上绑架他，说服詹姆斯道："他绝不会做伤害儿子的事，不是吗？"从本质上来说，如果詹姆斯的意见与长辈稍有偏离，就会被谴责。

"天主教会教导你要绝对听话，听从父母的要求。"詹姆斯说，"尊重是双向的，所以，年少的大部分时光里，我的观点都是被否定的。我的生活像一场噩梦，但同时也是幻想的世界，在那里我天真地被庇护着，与现实隔离。我的家庭待我像握瓷器一般，但他们把我握得太紧，使我最终崩溃了。他们的处理方式很大程度上是因为对我所受的煎熬都置之不理，特别是阿斯伯格综合征，在他们眼里我非常完美。"

因为詹姆斯是个健谈且社交活跃的孩子，所以几乎没有大人怀疑过他会有任何形式的自闭症。咿呀学步时的詹姆斯曾参

詹姆斯

加了蒙台梭利幼儿园,留下了许多最珍贵的回忆。但是,进入小学后,他的残疾开始显露出来了。

詹姆斯生动地回忆起与一位自恋的中学老师保尔森先生的对抗,"童年时,我一直有很多独特的兴趣,这是自闭症的常见症状,我们会注意力集中在一个特定主题上,百分之一百一地投入其中学习并享受它。当时我对超人的标志很着迷,所以在计算机课上花了很多时间用电脑去画。有一次,保尔森先生对我说希望我能尝试别的东西,然而,我并不想尝试其他的东西,所以一直在反复画。猜我的老师如何反应?他罚我离开电脑几分钟,让我把做错的事情写下来,并对我说在其他事情上'我对你太失望了'。但是他怎么能强迫我放弃当时喜欢的东西,让我去做不喜欢的事呢。还有一件事,每周我们都会去基督教青年会(Young Men's Christian Association,YMCA)游泳。一天,我不太想去游泳,并试图跟保尔森先生解释原因。你知道他做了什么吗?他威胁我要取消我喜欢的一些课程,比如计算机等,最终我去了游泳课。他竟然像父亲那样勒索我。人们觉得我对这所学校来说太完美了,所以会嫉妒我。总之,我感觉在公立学院的大部分时间都非常痛苦。"

显然,詹姆斯不断恶化的心理稳定程度也因被欺负而加重。詹姆斯回忆说:"我还是个孩子时,差不多六七八岁的样子,开始痴迷于麦当娜,因为当时她登上了行业巅峰。然而我的同

龄人几乎都是从父母辈那儿听说麦当娜的,所以他们会因此取笑我。他们认为麦当娜很糟糕,我辩解道:'别说了,她一点也不糟糕。'一天,三年级的老师试图教我,她问道:'詹姆斯,你喜欢布鲁斯斯普林斯汀吗?'我说:'不是很喜欢。'她说:'太伤心了,我有他所有的专辑。'我只是想表达:'嘿,他只不过不是我喜欢的那一类而已。'但我没向她表达清楚,她也没能理解我并没有贬低她的意思。然而其他孩子也开始落井下石,说:'麦当娜非常不好,麦当娜这样那样的。'他们仿佛要把麦当娜说成魔鬼。这让我在世界上感到非常孤独。"

詹姆斯的父母很好奇,为何生活幸福,儿子看起来却很另类。1996年,已是成熟少年的詹姆斯被确诊患有自闭症,当时还尚未分类,具体来说是阿斯伯格综合征,一种轻度的自闭症形式。之后便被带去看了大量的医生,但是父母从没告诉他为什么他总是被心理健康问题所冲击。"我很疑惑,为什么我们总是去看医生,看完医生后,我就会想自己是得什么病了吗?"詹姆斯回忆道。

出于关心,詹姆斯的父母向儿子隐瞒了实情,实际上他的整个童年都伴有阿斯伯格综合征。父母只是送他去看说话治疗师,从1996到2000年,这位专家一直在教詹姆斯与同龄人沟通。"因为在此之前,我总是自恋地谈论自己,所以我需要先听其他人说话,然后通过提问提取信息。这时,我的自闭症

和父亲带给我的家庭创伤之间的界限变得模糊了。当然，现在我会对别人的感受表现出兴趣，因为这是正确的。原来我从没有过真正的同理心，现在我学会了。虽然进步了，但我还是会回想起以前支离破碎的日子。"

之后，詹姆斯被送到了离家十五分钟距离的沃尔夫森学院，一所特殊教育学校。据他描述，每个教室有大约十个孩子，所有事物都"比平时更有趣"。在学校里，詹姆斯和同龄人融入到一起，重获了童年被夺走的自由感。

在18岁要独立的年纪上，詹姆斯在沃尔夫森学院待的很满足。几年前，他试图说服父亲帮他支付学唱歌的费用，提出他要模仿杰克逊、休斯顿等歌星，当然还有麦当娜。父亲对此想法表示蔑视，而是建议儿子去附近的一所大学。"父亲希望我完全成为他的复制品"。詹姆斯说，"但问题是，我不想上大学。学生可以在沃尔夫森待到21岁，我也想一直待到21岁。然而，父母硬逼我去上大学。他们说'尝试一下'。因此，我不得不去大学了，其间的整个经历都很痛苦。你知道吗？两年半后我退学了，他们对我说：'也许你应该留在沃尔夫森，不过至少已经尝试过大学了。'那时，家人从来没有为我打下过根基，我就像重压下的树枝，啪的一声突然折断。在这生命的关键时刻，我在想，家人在给予我庇护，强压给我那些不适当的或病态的活动之后，是如何做到这一切的。难道他们希望上帝突然将我

带走吗？这些绝对都是我父亲的所作所为。"

詹姆斯的父母在儿子生命的关键时刻，突然向他透漏了青年时期的秘密：他被诊断为阿斯伯格综合征。詹姆斯非常震惊，他一直觉得自己有些异样，但他从来没意识到这是受损伤的程度。加上对完美的不断期待，绝望与震惊的詹姆斯瘫在地上。"起初，我拒绝接受现实，然后感觉好像世界欠我的。"詹姆斯说，"我花了无数个夜晚去想自己为什么如此不同，而当从父母那儿得知这是因为自闭症的原因时，我崩溃了。这是生命中最糟糕的时刻，我开始表现得好像患有严重形式的自闭症。多希望能拿回年少时父母本来可以为我做的所有事，但他们却一直在掩盖，因为他们一直否认儿子不完美的这个事实。"因受情绪不稳定和 PTSD 的困扰，2003 年詹姆斯试图结束自己的生命。

虽然接受了住院治疗和门诊治疗（最终达到 8 次 ECT 治疗），詹姆斯还是在第二年患上了抑郁症。后来，他将这痛苦描述为"冰山一角"。尽管詹姆斯承认了自己患有阿斯伯格综合征，家里其他成员还是将这个诊断视为虚设。"我有个表姐，叫特里萨，她住在史坦顿岛。"詹姆斯说，"她试图在 Facebook 上宽慰我，你没有生病，没有生病，这是一种情感勒索的方式。而我平静地对她说：'特里萨，我已经被确诊了，确实有阿斯伯格综合征。'"

从根本上来说，詹姆斯康复的第一步是找一份工作。"找工作是一条漫长而坎坷的路。我刚在康复诊所度过了一段时间，

詹姆斯

为了避免精神崩溃，工作的灵活性和适合范围严格受限。但是工作教练确实帮了忙，他帮我一起制作简历。第一次，我尝试了一份在纽瓦克机场供餐的工作，因为住得太远，他们犹豫了要不要雇用我，于是我决定不去了。然后又申请了现在工作的绍普莱特，雇主很喜欢我的个性，聘请我为季节性工作人员，但最终由于财务状况不佳，我被辞退了。整个期间，我的情绪一直处于谷底。许多快乐的情绪稍纵即逝，而童年里悲伤的记忆却一直隐藏无法退去。有时，工作上会遇到困难，无法应对一些刁钻的客户。因为社交技能太差（因阿斯伯格综合征而感到受损），有时我会和同事争吵，或者甚至不知道自己侵犯了别人的私人空间。这种感觉就像在坐过山车一样，而且开始有作呕的感觉。"

詹姆斯希望能找到支持自己的伙伴，开始向更多陌生人敞开心扉。2010年，他遇到了男朋友马克，詹姆斯说马克就像"上帝所赐"。

"马克恰如其分地带来了光明，他挑战家人抚养我的方式，敢于和父亲开诚布公地分享他的观点。而我的家人认为马克想把我从他们身边带走。"在马克耐心的引导下，詹姆斯能够突破"很多自闭症的限制了，尽管他的心灵需要付出沉重代价"。

再次回到绍普莱特全职工作，詹姆斯意识到过去如何塑造了他今天的性格。"如果父母没有将我的残疾保密，我会学着

接受自己的另类。然而,现在的我被迫重温童年时期的恐惧,与PTSD共存。目前我仍和父亲住在一起。由于自闭症,我可以通过医疗保险和社会残疾保障接受政府的资助,但可惜的是,我必须以残疾人的身份才能获得这些经济资助。当父亲2010年退休后,我就可以凭退休人员供养残疾人的原因接受更多资助,但老实说,我只想自己住。虽然我不符合申请公共房屋的条件,但我希望能生活得没有阻碍,卸下过去的创伤。"

詹姆斯望着窗外,讲述了生命中最伟大的时刻,那就是遇到格伦·斯卡普利时。跟自己一样,格伦来自史坦顿岛,是意大利人,也是同性恋。一月份,当詹姆斯开始看20世纪80年代的电视剧《活在当下(One Day at a Time)》时,便被格伦在剧中饰演的亚历克斯·克里斯里克所迷住。詹姆斯回忆说,一时兴起,他就在Facebook上给格伦发了消息。令他感到惊讶的是,格伦回复了,他告诉詹姆斯下个月会在当地的一个剧院举行见面会。实际上,格伦为詹姆斯起了一个昵称:"他同性恋伙伴的名字:斯塔恩·艾兰德"。在活动的前一周,詹姆斯便按捺不住了,无法抑制自己的兴奋。"我不想让格伦认为我是一个疯狂的跟踪者。所以我在想,该如何表现,他才不那么想?幸运的是,我去到那儿时,表现非常好。当我介绍自己是Facebook中的斯塔恩·艾兰德时,他的脸色为之一亮,我永远都会记得这个瞬间。他见到我很高兴,我原本希望可以拥抱一下他,其实

詹姆斯

我根本没必要担心,因为他从座位上跳了起来拥抱我,我们俩就像老朋友一样。当时格伦已经年过五十,我还从来没有迷恋过五十岁的人,但格伦不一样。"说着詹姆斯拿出手机找到了一张记录他们会面的照片。左边的是格伦,身穿一件清新的蓝色衬衫,詹姆斯穿着一件亮黄色T恤,他右手挽着格伦,两个人都笑容满面。詹姆斯说,"这些瞬间让生活变得特别。跟格伦聊天会让我得到宣泄,特别是在因自闭症或PTSD而挣扎、煎熬时,我只记得格伦热情洋溢的脸,这些我会永远珍惜!"

# Emily

Living 2,500 miles away from home. Balancing a rigorous course load at a liberal arts college. At only 20 years old, Emily has projected herself as a capable and independent student, who, despite her autism, has maintained a balanced life. Past her success, much of which can be accredited to her mother, however, lies years of turbulence, involving heated lawsuits against the school district and persistent qualms about the future.

Ms. Fonda, Emily's mother, told us how her daughter's journey began: "We were in church one morning-Emily and me-sitting around a table for lunch. I noticed that across the room, this woman who had been attending Mass with me kept peering over at Emily. When I caught her glance, she approached me. For being mere acquaintances, she was very

Emily

blunt. She said, 'I think your child has autism.'

"As anyone would be, I was offended at first. I had known autism was more common in boys than in girls, so, since Emily was a girl, her accusation was all the more jarring. Eventually, I thought, it wouldn't hurt to rule out the possibility of autism. Then the woman might stop bothering me. So, I asked my doctor to find help for Emily, but since my insurance company limited the referrals he could give me, I ended up having to visit a speech therapist, and later a neurodevelopmental pediatrician."

Simply scheduling an appointment was difficult. "When I called the pediatrician's office, the receptionist told me it would be months until Emily would be checked. I said, 'Six months? Crazy.' So I had Emily put on the waiting list. And I didn't just stop there. Every three days I called the doctor, hoping and praying for someone to cancel an appointment. Soon, they told me there was an opening, and I snatched it right away."

At the time Emily was diagnosed with autism, Ms. Fonda was in the hospital, giving birth to her second son Paul. When her husband and daughter came back from the doctor's clinic that afternoon, Ms. Fonda remembers, "They said nothing! My

husband just ambled into the room and sat down beside me. It wasn't until that night when I asked him what the pediatrician had said, that he handed me the diagnosis sheet."

Like most parents, Ms. Fonda was shocked. Immediately, she called the professional Dr. Webster, and using her "limited knowledge of autism," started arguing, "Autistic children don't have eye contact, well Emily does have eye contact! Autistic children can't interact with other, well Emily talks to her family members!"

"I was spitting out everything I knew about autism to refute the diagnosis, but Dr. Webster responded calmly. She said, 'Yes, Emily can look at you, but there is something missing in her eyes.'"

Even though I was even more confused by Dr. Webster's explanation, that afternoon, I took her words into consideration. It was the exact moment that Emily looked at her baby brother that I noticed something was off. Maybe my daughter was autistic. My niece Susan gazed at Paul with love and affection while Emily stared blankly at Paul as if he were a toy. Her eyes were empty. Slowly, I let down my guard, and when I searched the web for more information about autism, I realized that

Emily

Emily had displayed so many symptoms of autism I had been too ignorant to acknowledge."

Ms. Fonda originally home-schooled Emily for two years, before considering a specialized school. The Glass Disability Center-nearby. She wanted to ensure her school district could provide Emily with adequate support ranging up to $90,000. When she approached the superintendent and presented Emily's case to him, he tried to deny the diagnosis, flattering, 'But your daughter is so beautiful, how could you put such a nasty label on her?'

Ms. Fonda asserted, "I don't care about the label. No label, no services. It's not that I want her to be autistic."

"I told them it was hard for me to accept Emily's diagnosis as well, but he and his team maintained that they could not fund Emily. So, I had to confirm the diagnosis with a specialized institute and warned the district, 'You don't want to have an IEP meeting with me. I've taken Emily to this respected professional, and I have even confirmed what my medical doctor has said.' They knew right away that if they had that meeting, within 15 days, they would be fined for violating New Jersey Law."

Navigating Transitions
风雨同舟

Finally, the school district complied and Ms. Fonda made it her obligation to learn as much as she could about autism. This knowledge, she realized, would allow her to advocate strongly on Emily's behalf. Upon attending a conference, in fact, she met with the Glass Disability Center director, Dr. Shannon, and learned some startling information-Emily had consistently been placed in wrong classes, and on purpose.

"I went through the old files and realized something was wrong. I immediately emailed the special education director, and Dr. Shannon identified multiple areas in which our school was violating the law. He sent someone to call us informing, 'You need to take your district to court, and don't file due process because the time you see the judge, it'll be a month or two months later; instead, file emergency release hearing. Within five calendar days, the judge will take your hearing. Our district knew that they did not have any grounds, that they kept dragging their feet. That maybe because I was a minority, they thought I would succumb to their wishes. I had been friendly with them, sending them Christmas gifts, Thanksgiving gifts, just hanging on to the hope that they could help my daughter. But nothing had happened. Emily could not wait."

Emily

"I hated to take the district to court-it's just not my nature-so I filed for a hearing. Before sending the papers out, though, I still felt that I could give them another chance to work together. I didn't want an adversary. So, I dropped the petition on the desk of the superintendent. Within 20 minutes-and keep in mind I had been emailing her and calling her every day before and getting no response, and after I dropped that and wrote a note that said 'Dr. Westbrook, I would hate to take this step, though I have been intensely advised by the Department of Education to do so-I got my response. She said, 'We accept Emily's diagnosis, and you know what, I promise you when the New Year comes, you will have an IEP meeting.' And I believed them."

After the winter break, Ms. Fonda met with Dr. Westbrook for an IEP meeting. Ms. Fonda had hoped Emily could attend the Glass Disability Center, but after a short conversation, realized that since perspective students were enrolled in the fall, there was little chance Emily would be considered in late January.

"Admittance to the Glass Disability Center is lower than admittance to Harvard. One class only has six students, and

the staff to student ratio is phenomenal-one to one. So you can see how great this school is. When Dr. Westbrook told me that this option was closed to Emily, I said, 'I don't think that's my fault now. When this school had an opening, I was pleading that you hear my case. If you had listened, Emily could be attending at this moment!' The Glass Disability Center loved Emily and could really spot her potential; unfortunately, their next opening was in the following summer."

Ms. Fonda was troubled for her daughter's future and pushed the school to start a home-school program dedicated to Emily.

"I told them: I will work with you, but I will not give up. I will not give in. Because I know that early treatment is essential to the brain. So the school gave me a home program, even though we had already brought in therapists into our home. Then, they complained again, 'Ms. Fonda, it is so hard to find therapists. It might take a while.' and I exclaimed,

'Great, I already have therapists that help Emily so we can just use mine.' The difference now was that before we had to pay these aids; after, the district paid for them."

The school board provided up to 25 hours of weekly

Emily

services to Emily, such as speech therapy for $120 per hour (the charge in 1999). Support provided past the 25 hour threshold was covered by the Fong family. Through an unexpected turn of events, Emily was actually progressing faster than most of her peers. The sound basis for learning and development offered by at-home therapists served as an advantage.

Although most of her conflicts with the district had been resolved, Ms. Fonda still had frequent altercations with her case manager.

"During my research, I studied Applied Behavioral Analysis (ABA), which is a very hands-on intervention that brings out lots of positive behaviors for children with autism. I called my case manager, saying 'Emily needs this.' His response: 'Do you know what is ABA? That is a method tried on animals, to train them!' But I didn't care, as long as ABA could help my daughter! He was trained to delay things, to dispel knowledgeable parents."

Soon after, when Dr. Shannon joined Ms. Fonda's IEP team-Ms. Fonda, unlike the district, could afford Dr. Shannon's costly services-he advocated on her behalf: "I help children on the spectrum in and out with ABA. I know it works."

Unable to counter Westbrook's testimony, the school district offered Ms. Fonda ABA treatment through the 25 hours weekly services.

The next year, Emily was taken off the Glass Disability Center waiting list and enrolled in the Glass School. Ms. Fonda finally had some stability, with "no litigations having to be involved."

"This was the peaceful time of my life. Everything went smoothly. But it wasn't long until we had to integrate back into the school district and from 2002 to 2008, we had to take the school to court every year to have an ABA trained therapist continuing to work with Emily. People were so tired of it all, but it was all indispensable. I never gave up. It was like I was rowing a boat against a current, and if we weren't progressing, we were regressing. I am a neuroscientist, so I knew that the brain could be reshaped when it is very young. We were in a race against time."

Ms. Fonda decided to represent Emily in court. The litigation fee was already more than the services she was requesting and hiring a lawyer would only add on to the costs.

"Our last due process, in the hearing at the end, a judge

Emily

came to see me. Not just because I had gone to court so many times, but because I had also started fighting for other parents. The entire court had heard about me at this point! I told him I would not stop until Emily was given proper help. I had reached out to the Department of Education even, and I got a reply from Obama, telling me to settle. The judge asked me what I wanted and told him the amount of money. He gasped, 'That little?' But I wasn't trying to bankrupt the school district, though I certainly could have asked for more. After all, they had spent $100,000 trying to fight me for two years. That's just ridiculous. I wanted to get back to my life."

Ms. Fonda's dedication and hard work certainly paid off. With the concentrated help from therapists and tutors, Emily's development was phenomenal. For her annual evaluation, the doctor determined that her age equivalence moved two years ahead in only six months.

One afternoon, when Emily was in sixth grade, she asked her mother, "Why did I go to the Glass Center when my friend Ruth went to the preschool next to our house?" Taken aback by Emily's sudden curiosity, Ms. Fonda was unsure how to respond.

"At the time, I told Emily that she had autism. I wanted to be the one to tell her about her autism, and not for her to hear from other kids. But what I should have done is just tell her the symptoms of autism. Autism gave her a label. She started to remember all the signs on the highways and advocacy campaigns in our county, how they claimed that there was no cure for autism. She was embarrassed, especially since all my friends knew they couldn't escape Ms. Fonda without a bit of autism knowledge. After that, I was more careful not to be so public about Emily's autism, so I did more things behind the scenes."

When she was in eighth grade, Emily transferred to a Christian private school, where the staff was amiable, and plenty of support was available. Since her husband had started a company in Japan and no longer lived with the family, Ms. Fonda had to "choose her battles."

"The teachers there were all Christian, and I didn't ask for too much. All Emily needed was a textbook to be sent home and a bus stop by our house that's it! We still paid for Emily's therapy and after intensive treatments every summer, she became the class valedictorian in both middle school and high

Emily

school."

When Emily started searching for colleges, she stumbled across a selective liberal arts school in California. With its small student body and scenic campus, the college immediately attracted Emily's attention. She wanted a closed-environment dedicated to learning, and the school satisfied all her needs. Upon applying early to the college, she was one of just 160 students accepted.

"She managed well pursuing higher education because the faculty was so renowned and the grading system allowed for low test scores to be curved to As and Bs. During her freshmen year, she even got an internship with Microsoft, and without mentioning her autism! Even though I know that she would be qualified for many more scholarships if Emily states she has autism, since these accolades have a different baseline, I respect my daughter's decision to keep her disability private. She is sensitive in this regard."

Overall, Emily has thrived at college. For the past two semesters, she has studied abroad in China and Budapest and has taken full responsibility for her own life. In a letter she wrote her mom: Don't be concerned. I'm doing great.

While facilitating her daughter growth was grueling, Ms. Fonda has no regrets. Her efforts molded Emily into an independent and mature woman.

And she's learned a lot in the process: "Be willing to accept your child's autism and face it. Don't be in denial. Be your child's best advocate. Be savvy with the law and services your child needs. And don't miss the most precious times just to help. I didn't wait. Autism treatment is expensive, but if your family can afford to go cruising, then you can afford treatment! Our family didn't go on vacation for so many years because we'd rather channel our resources to Emily."

# 艾米莉

刚刚二十岁的艾米莉,在一所离家两千多英里的文科大学读书,很好地平衡着严密的课程负担。此时的她已经成长为有才华、独立的大学生,虽然患有自闭症,却也过着平衡的生活。艾米莉过去大部分的成功可谓归功于她的母亲,殊不知,她们经历了多年的波折动荡,有对学区(属于美国的地方政府)激烈的控诉,也有对未来不断的焦虑。

艾米莉的母亲方达女士清晰地记得女儿的艰难之路是如何开始的:"那天早上,艾米莉和我在教堂里,围坐在桌子旁吃早餐。我注意到,房间那头一个和跟我一起参加了两三年教堂活动的女人,直盯着艾米莉看。我俩目光相视时候,她走近我,因为不是很熟,她说得很直接:'我觉得你的孩子患有自闭症。'"

"像大多数人一样,开始我很生气。据我所知,自闭症在男孩中的发病率比在女孩中要高,但艾米莉是女孩,这让她的断言变得尤为刺耳。最后,我想,如果能排除自闭症的可能性

也没有坏处，可能这样那个女人就不会再打扰到我了。于是，我请医生来帮艾米莉，但因为医生所提供的转诊医院受保险公司的限制，所以不得不转而去拜访一位说话治疗师，之后是一位神经发育儿科医生。"

单独安排一场会诊比较困难。"我给儿科医生办公室打电话时，前台告诉我安排艾米莉检查可能要等上几个月。我反问道：'几个月？这也太长了。'所以我们登记在了等待名单中。我并没有就这样放弃，每隔三天给医生打一次电话，祈祷着希望有人能取消预约。很快，医院告诉我有一个空缺，我马上抓住了机会。"

艾米莉确诊患有自闭症时，方达女士在医院生下了她的第二个儿子保罗。当天下午丈夫和女儿从医生诊所回来时，她回忆道："他们什么都没有说！我的丈夫慢慢走进房间，在我旁边坐下。直到当天晚上，我问他儿科医生怎么说，他才将诊断书递给我。"

跟大多数父母一样，方达女士震惊了。她马上打电话给专家韦伯斯特博士，并用自己"仅有的关于自闭症的知识"开始辩解："自闭症儿童是不会跟人有眼神交流的，而艾米莉会有眼神交流！自闭症儿童不会跟其他人有沟通，而艾米莉会跟家人交谈！"

"我几乎穷尽了所有自己知道的关于自闭症的知识去反驳

艾米莉

这个诊断,但韦伯斯特博士冷静地回答:'没错,艾米莉是会看你,但她的眼神中丢失了一些东西。'"

"尽管我仍然对韦伯斯特博士的解释感到困惑,不过那天下午我开始认真思考她的话了。当艾米莉看她的小弟弟时,我才注意到有什么东西不对劲,可能我女儿患上自闭症了。我侄女苏珊充满爱意地看着保罗,而艾米莉面无表情地盯着保罗,仿佛他是一个玩具,目光空洞。我开始慢慢卸下盔甲。后来,我在网上查了很多自闭症的相关信息,突然意识到,可怕的是,艾米莉已经表现出了许多自闭症的症状,只不过因为我的无知甚至从没考虑过这些问题。"

起初,在考虑接受学区服务之前,方达女士让艾米莉在家学了两年。认识到资助自闭症儿童的巨大开支后,她希望确保学校能为艾米莉提供足够的支持,起码能在90000美元以上。当她联系学区总监,并把艾米莉的情况介绍给他时,总监试图否认这个诊断,恭维道:"你女儿这么漂亮,怎么能给她贴上这样一个标签呢?"

方达女士肯定地说:"我不在意标签,不是这个标签,我们也不会需要服务。这是医生的诊断,不是我想让她得自闭症。"

"我告诉他们,自己也很难接受艾米莉的诊断结果,但他们依旧不肯资助艾米莉,所以我必须请一家专业的机构——玻璃残障中心(Glass Disability Center)确认诊断结果,然后提醒

Navigating Transitions
风雨同舟

地区政府:'你们不愿意跟我开 IEP(个别化教育计划)会议,所以我带艾米莉到这家权威专业机构证实了医生的诊断。'他们立刻明白如果举行 IEP 会议,十五天内将会因违反新泽西州法律而被处罚。"

最终,学区默许,而方达女士把学习自闭症当作自己的义务,尽可能地多学。她意识到,这些知识能让她代表艾米莉有力地维护自己的主张。在一次会议上,她见到了玻璃残障中心的主任香农博士,了解到一些令人震惊的消息,原来艾米莉一直被有意安排上着不合适的课程。

"我浏览了些旧文件,意识到有些不对,立即通过邮件发给特殊教育主任,香农博士指出女儿所在的学校违反了多个法律领域。他派人打电话告诉我们:'你需要把地区政府告上法庭,但不要申请正常程序,因为这样的话可能一两个月后才能见到法官;相反,申请紧急召开听证会。法官会在五日内听取你的证词。'地区政府知道自己没有任何理由,因此一直拖延。他们以为我是少数群体,所以会屈服于他们的志愿。一直以来,我都很友善,给他们送圣诞礼物、感恩节礼物,只希望他们能尽心帮助我女儿。但事实并没有,我不能再等下去了。"

"我不愿跟地区政府对簿公堂,这也不是我的本意,所以我申请了听证会。然而,发送申请之前,我仍觉得应该再给他们一次合作的机会,因为我不想与任何人树敌。所以我把诉状

艾米莉

放到了学区总监的办公桌上。之前我一再给他发邮件打电话都没有得到任何回复,但诉状放到他桌上,并留言道:'韦斯特布鲁克博士,尽管教育局多次建议我申请诉讼,但我非常不想走这一步。'之后,不到二十分钟就收到了回复,她说:'我们承认艾米莉的诊断结果,也答应你新年过后,我们会召集一次 IEP 会议'。我相信了他们。"

寒假过后,方达女士去见韦斯特布鲁克博士并出席 IEP 会议。原本方达女士希望艾米莉能加入玻璃残障中心,但经过短暂交谈后,她意识到新生都是秋季入学,所以艾米莉一月底能入学的几率非常低。

"进入玻璃残障中心比被哈佛录取稍微容易一些。一个班只有六名学生,师生比为一比一,十分惊人。所以你就知道这所学校有多厉害了。韦斯特布鲁克博士告诉我艾米莉不能选这个学校时,我反驳道:'我不认为现在错在我,可以申请学校时,我恳求你听听我的情况。如果当时你听了,艾米莉这时就有可能入学了。'玻璃残障中心是爱艾米莉的,能真正发现她的潜力;遗憾的是,下次开学要等到夏天了。"

方达女士对女儿的未来深感担忧,她开始推动学校为艾米莉开设家庭学校课程。

"我告诉他们:我会和你们一起努力,决不放弃。因为我知道早期治疗对智力非常重要,所以是不会退让的。尽管我们

已经请了家庭治疗师，还是学校来提供家庭方案，但他们又抱怨道：'方达女士，找治疗师非常困难，这需要一点时间。'我大声说道：'很好，我已经找到了帮助艾米莉的治疗师，所以可以用我们找的。'现在的区别是，之前我们自己付钱，现在由地区政府为此买单。"

教育委员会相当于每周为艾米莉提供 25 小时的服务支持，例如每小时 120 美元的说话治疗（1999 年的收费）。超出 25 小时之外的服务费需由方家自行承担。事实上，事情的意外转折使艾米莉比大部分同龄人进步得更快，这得益于家庭治疗师为其学习和发展打下的坚实基础。

尽管与地区政府的冲突大部分解决了，但方达女士和个案经理还是冲突频发。

"通过研究，我学习了应用行为分析法（Applied Behavioral Analysis，ABA），特别需要人工干预，能激发自闭症儿童许多积极的行为。我打电话给我们的个案经理，说'艾米莉需要进行 ABA 治疗'。他回道：'你懂什么是 ABA 吗？这是一种尝试训练动物的方法！'但我不在乎，只要 ABA 可以帮到我女儿！个案经理向来只会把事情往后拖，劝退学识渊博的家长们。"

不久之后，香农博士加入了方达女士的 IEP 小组，跟地区政府不同，方达女士付给香农博士高薪，他替方达女士辩解道：

艾米莉

"我帮很多儿童做过 ABA，确实有效。"学区无法反驳他的证言，于是在每周 25 小时的服务中为艾米莉提供了 ABA 治疗。

第二年，艾米莉被拿下玻璃残障中心的候补名单，进入了玻璃学校。方达女士终于摆脱了诉讼，稳定了一些。

"那时一切进展顺利，是我生命中难得的宁静时光。但好景不长，2002 年到 2008 年，我们又要重新归入学区，几乎每年都要把学校送上法庭，只为了找到一位训练有素的 ABA 治疗师能持续跟艾米莉一起。其他人都已对此感到厌倦了，但这一切非常必要，我从未放弃过。就像逆水行舟，不进则退。我是一位神经系统科学家，所以我知道人在年幼时大脑是可以重塑的。我们在跟时间赛跑。"

方达女士决定代表艾米莉出庭，诉讼费已经比她要求的服务所需费用要多，而且加上律师费，费用只多不减。

"听证会的尾声，也就是最后一道程序时，一位法官来看我。不仅因为我去过法庭很多次，还因为我也是在为其他家庭的父母而战。从这点而言，整个法庭就都已经知晓我了。我告诉他，我不会停下来的，直到艾米莉得到恰当的帮助。我甚至找到了教育部，并得到了奥巴马的回复，他告诉我会解决的。问我想要什么，我告诉他我需要一笔钱。他热切地问：'就只有这些？'我当然可以要求更多，但我也不是想让学区破产。说起来也可笑，毕竟学区曾花了 100000 美元跟我打了两年的官司。我只想回到

正常的生活。"

"这样做是值得的,我所在的地区政府一直以来都拒绝提供这些服务,推迟执行。现在,因为我的努力让他们知道了坚持不懈的父母会怎样。"

方达女士的巨大付出和艰苦努力确实得到了回报。在治疗师和教师全力以赴的帮助下,艾米莉的进步是惊人的。经过年终检查,医生确定她的相对年龄只用了六个月就增长了两岁。

在读六年级时的一个下午,艾米莉问妈妈:"为什么我的朋友露丝去上咱们家旁边的幼儿园,而我要去残疾中心?"艾米莉突如其来的好奇使她大吃一惊,方达女士不知道如何回答。

"当时,我告诉艾米莉她有自闭症。我希望由我来告诉她自闭症,而不是从其他孩子那儿听来。但我能做的只是告诉她自闭症的症状。自闭症给了她一个标签,在看到郡里高速公路上和倡议活动中的内容后她开始思考,为什么他们说自闭症无法治愈。她感到尴尬,尤其是在我向所有朋友都普及过自闭症知识之后。因此,我更加注意尽量避免在公众场合提及艾米莉的自闭症。所以在幕后做了更多努力。"

艾米莉八年级时转学到了一所基督私立学校,那里工作人员和蔼可亲,能提供大量支持。因为丈夫在日本开了一家公司,不能和家人住一起了,所以方达女士不得不相应调整。

"那里的老师都是基督徒,我也没有太多要求。艾米莉所

需要的就是帮她把课本一起送到我家门前的公共汽车站点。我们仍在付费为艾米莉治疗，经过多个夏天的强化治疗，她成为了初中和高中毕业典礼上优秀的毕业生代表。"

当艾米莉开始搜索大学时，她偶然发现加利福尼亚的一所文科学校还不错。学校学生人数不多，校园风景优美，很快便吸引了艾米莉的注意。她想要一个可以专注于学习的封闭环境，而这所学校满足了她所有的需求。在早期申请者中，学校录取了160位学生，艾米莉就在其中。

"那里的教师非常知名，而且评分系统允许考试分数低的学生拿到A和B，所以在这里接受高等教育的艾米莉做得还不错。大一期间，她甚至得到了微软的实习机会，但是没有提及她的自闭症。即便我明白，艾米莉如果说出她患有自闭症，就会因这些评比对残疾人所设标准较低而获得更多奖学金，但我还是尊重女儿的决定，为她的残疾保密。她在这方面非常敏感。"

总体来说，艾米莉在大学里成长了很多。前两个学期，她还到中国和布达佩斯留学，自己全权照料自己的生活，在给妈妈的一封信中写到：不要担心，我很好。

尽管帮女儿成长的过程十分煎熬，方达女士却没有遗憾。她的努力将艾米莉塑造成一个独立而成熟的女人。

而且，在这个过程中方达女士学到了很多东西："不要否认，而是去接受孩子患有自闭症的事实，敢于面对。做孩子最好的

支持者,要精通孩子所需要的法律和服务支持。不要错过寻求帮助的最佳时间,我从不等待。自闭症治疗费非常贵,但是如果一个家庭能够负担得起旅行开支,那么就可以负担得起治疗费用!我们家很多年都没有度过假了,因为想把更多的资源留给艾米莉。"

# Dylan

What defines an individual's journey with autism? For Dylan Sanders, his experiences with PDD have always been marked by the unexpected.

20 years ago, autism was not well understood, as it is today and when Dylan first received his diagnosis at three years old, there lacked the adequate resources to aid his difficulties with speech.

Ms. Sanders didn't know anything about autism, expect for what [she] saw from the movie *Rainman* and was confused by her son's reticence and his backward progress. Before, Dylan had an insatiable appetite. Gradually, he became a picky eater and started losing interest in different foods. Likewise, Dylan once enjoyed playing with a chest of toys but started fixating on a single rubber ball.

Even his communication deteriorated. "When he talked to you, it would just be clips of what the actors said on TV. If Barney said, 'Today's going to be a beautiful day!' he would respond, 'today's going to be a beautiful day!' when I asked him how his day had gone. You could understand what he meant, but it was clear that it was just his method of speaking."

"He wasn't talking and using words the same-not forming sentences. He used to be always content and happy. He could just be happy all day. I wish it were just one thing so I could identify his autism and so I could have explained it to my doctor, who thought I was crazy. The doctor said to me, 'There's nothing wrong with Dylan,' and I maintained, 'No, there is definitely something different about him.' I just knew. There was too much progressing not at the same level."

Feeling uneasy, Ms. Sanders researched additional consulting in her area and scheduled an appointment with a specialized hospital. There, the staff confirmed her suspicions: Dylan had autism.

"I'm an engineer, so I like to solve things quickly. Soon afterward, I reached out to Good Shepherd, a program that

Dylan

could support Dylan. The organization's doctor had experience working with children on the autism spectrum and introduced me to occupational therapists and treatment options to initiate early intervention."

"The early intervention program was similar to a preschool because we took Dylan to the center every day. As a family, we definitely made the right decision. It took a lot of effort on our end, but the earlier the treatment starts, the less stress parents have in the future. There was a plethora of resources there that we were able to use, and the teachers were incredibly patient as well."

"What has helped my son over the years are definitely the mentors, who aren't just limited to professionals, of course. Dylan always emulated his sister, who is four years older than him. I think from younger ages to all the way up, having somebody with him helped him grow his motor skills. One-on-one teaching helped a personalized aid. Overall, having someone there to show him, to remind him the right thing to do provided him instant feedback that would correct his behavior."

In particular, being paired with Ms. Lee, a special education instructor from elementary through middle school

was "pivotal to his development."

Such continuity reassured Dylan and strengthened the teacher-student bond. "She kept in constant contact with me and was always coming up with new things to try, new things to change. It was customized, personal, in this sense. That was what changed his life, no doubt. This constant support system even allowed him to take classes outside the special education department, which was a huge feat for us."

As the semester drew to a close and Dylan move onto sixth grade, his mother made a big decision: to hold him back a year. Dylan had passed all his IEPs and was set to graduate from elementary school. Yet, Ms. Sanders noticed that he was a year behind in math and almost two years behind in language arts.

"I said to the school board, 'Shouldn't we have him repeat the fifth grade, so he has a chance to be caught up on his academics?' At first, the administration was hesitant, but I insisted, 'I've never had to get a lawyer, you guys have always cooperated. Listen to me, socially the kids in Dylan's class are a year behind, and it gives my son a chance to have a solid understanding of what is being taught.' By standing up for my son, I got my way. Had Dylan moved on the to middle school, I

Dylan

don't think he could have handled the pressure and workload."

The following year, Dylan enjoyed his mainstreamed classes but often had difficulties maintaining proper behavior. Recognizing this issue, Ms. Lee established a reminder system for Dylan with popsicle sticks. Whenever Dylan "acted-out," Ms. Lee would place a popsicle stick in a mason jar. Once the jar held three sticks, Dylan would have to spend more time back in the special education classes, and "he didn't want that." It was an effective strategy: Dylan was motivated to check his behavior.

"A good teacher is supposed to help your child learn while employing necessary discipline. In this regard, Ms. Lee was the best possible. She figured out Dylan was spending a lot of time in the bathroom to avoid going to class, so she said to me, 'This is going to sound cruel, but I'm only going to allow him seven passes for the rest of the day.' I said 'seven?' and she responded, 'Trust me, once I give him any pass, he is reminded and goes, never mind I don't have to go to the bathroom.' The consistency and personalization of it are what was key."

Although Ms. Lee was a reliable teacher, she wasn't a

suitable friend. Marcus, a popular classmate, willing to sit with Dylan during lunch, fulfilled this role instead.

"To this day Marcus still talks to my son. Having that role model and feeling of acceptance is just huge. To not always being with the special ed kids, but to actually feel like you're living a 'normal life.' "

"Overall, Dylan doesn't have much of a social life. The only friends he makes are through community service. By participating in clubs, where members go on day trips, he gets the opportunity to meet new people. He works on school plays, lends a hand to the lighting crew and surrounds himself with people. Dylan's innocence and positivity attract others. His Facebook posts, for one, are all about kindness."

With friendship a low priority in his life, Dylan concentrated on attending college. His mother, proud of her son, sought more independence, believing that if Dylan wanted to go, he should. His father, however, wanted Dylan to stay at home until he turned 21.

"My husband was afraid that if Dylan failed in college, he would have no more available services. I argued, 'You know, Dylan's doing well in school and if he wants to go, just let him.'

Dylan

To really assure that Dylan would have the best possible time at college, I even hired a college counselor Maria to assure Dylan would optimize his time at college. Her job was to travel to colleges and meet with their departments. Maria talked to their students and understood the way they gave support. Ultimately, she met with Dylan's teachers and narrowed a list of colleges that had the most comfortable learning environment for him."

On his college application, Dylan had to indicate his prospective major. He accumulated a list of interests and narrowed his focus on hotel services since he "had always enjoyed how the hotels would make visitors feel welcome." Having applied to ten colleges, he was accepted into a small university in Maine as a part of their one-year preparatory program. The university was geared toward students who needed extra academic help and offered them the opportunity to pursue a degree.

"The specific program Dylan was in had about 30 students. They had curfews, study halls, and as long as they were doing well in school, they would be weaned off these restrictions. The goal by the end of the year was to have complete independence. The college offered many levels of

support, although, with each increased level of support, the more money went out of our pockets."

Dylan's tutors explained his assignments and kept him on task. He was a competitive student, fulfilling all his credits, and not only graduated a semester early but also magna cum laude. The ceremony, Ms. Sanders claims, was a remarkable milestone.

"What really made Dylan's transition from high school to college easy was: number one, his active involvement in all the school activities. He was able to engage with a wide variety of people who were different like he was; he stayed busy. From drama club to hospitality club, he tried everything. Second, he loved independence and the support of the school. Whenever he came back home, his speech, his clarity, his confidence, were all wonderful. But the longer he stayed with us, not doing much, he started to lose much of that. Lastly, since Dylan doesn't like the uncertainty of life, college gave him a tight schedule to follow."

Besides his involvement in extracurriculars at the University, Dylan worked as an intern in a nearby hotel, and though he handled "crappy work," he didn't seem to mind.

Dylan

"Most people, when they go into internships, they try to do some observation and talk to people. Personally, I wish Dylan could have been more curious. If the staff had him make the bed, and get the keys, he was happy to have done just that. When I said to him, 'Did you learn what a front desk manager does?' and he replied, 'No, not really.' "

Training programs, ones at Hyatt, were worthwhile. After an interview and acceptance letter, Dylan was assigned to "work for 90 crazy days." He learned a scope of skills-from making a Long Island Ice Tea, working the front desk and brewing coffee and lattes. When visitors would ring for room service at midnight, Dylan was the employee to take their order, cook and deliver their meal. Unfortunately, Dylan was unable to pass a test to distinguish if guests were inebriated, and was denied a full-time position.

"What he learned from this experience was that if he needed help, he shouldn't be afraid to ask. It's OK to tell people that you have autism and what that means for you. You should just explain what that means for you-that's you're very, very good at doing work, as long as you understand the work, even if this requires a little extra help understanding. That you'll be

Navigating Transitions
风雨同舟

dependable and you'll love your job."

Moreover, Dylan learned to make better use of his job coach, who was in charge of finding local companies to "train Dylan and give him a chance." From their collaboration, Dylan is now working through Occupational Vocational Rehabilitation (OVR), a government agency, where he has undergone additional training through Holiday Inn. Since the stint is unpaid, Dylan is funded by OVR.

Dylan has also juggled several summer internships since his graduation from university, such as custodial duties at Dorney Park. To the surprise of his family, Dylan never complained about his job, even though he had to take out garbage and clean toilets in torrid weather.

"What kept him so eager was the fact that he could help people. He felt some sense of affirmation making people smile, directing strangers to the right rides, cleaning up after them. Since his boss understands his autism diagnosis, he is sure to congratulate Dylan often and make him feel comfortable. There were some rare off-days in which Dylan would come back home and would be talking to himself. When old habits would resurface, I encouraged Dylan to take a break. It was critical

that Dylan balance with health and work."

Currently, Dylan shares a home with his father, where he lives comfortably in the basement. With a bathroom, kitchen and a lounge, the space has given Dylan responsibility and has served as a simulation of a more independent lifestyle, his ultimate goal.

"We've discussed his future several times, and Dylan has expressed that he would like to get a roommate, share bills and move out on his own. Times when Dylan is nervous or anxious about this next chapter, we tell him, 'The struggles you go through are not just struggles that people with autism have. Everyone has hardships, and you just have to keep working through it. That is the mentality."

Reflecting upon her son's journey with autism, Mrs. Sanders says, "I had no idea what the future was going to look like. At all. I mean, never in my life did I think that we would be having my son at college, working, any of these things. There is just so much about loving our children with autism and getting past the worry all the time. Because, honestly, I'm constantly amazed."

# 迪伦

自闭症患者的人生该如何定义？对于迪伦·桑德斯来说，他的自闭症之路可谓一直充满意外和惊喜。

二十年前"自闭症还不像今天这样为人熟知"，三岁的迪伦接受了第一次诊断，当时没有充足的资源帮他克服交流的困难。

而他的母亲除了从电影《雨人》中看到的情节之外，对自闭症一无所知，只是她对儿子的安静程度和"倒退发展"感到疑惑。之前，迪伦胃口很大。渐渐地，他开始变得挑食，也不像之前对各种食物都那么感兴趣了。同样，曾经热衷于一整箱玩具的迪伦开始变得只盯着一个橡皮球转圈。

甚至他的沟通能力也开始恶化。"他跟你说话时，就像电视上的演员剪辑的片段。比如，巴尼说：'今天会是美好的一天！'迪伦同样会回答：'今天会是美好的一天！'"当我问他今天过得如何时，也只是勉强能明白他的意思。很明显，他的说话方式很奇特。

迪伦

"他不是在说话,而是在重复相同的词语,没办法表达出完整的句子。他总是满足和快乐的,有时竟能乐上一整天。我多希望只通过这一件事我就能辨认出他的自闭症,然后可以解释给医生。不过,医生认为我疯了,告诉我说:'迪伦一切正常。'但我还是坚持:'不,他一定是出了什么问题。'我很确信,因为他有太多方面的发展没有在同一个水平。"

不安的桑德斯夫人很快调查了当地其他咨询机构,并预约了一家专科医院。在那里,工作人员证实了她的怀疑:迪伦患有自闭症。

"我是一名工程师,所以喜欢快速解决问题。不久之后,我就与 Good Shepherd(善牧中心)取得联系,这里可以为迪伦提供支持。该机构有一位在儿童自闭症方面经验丰富的医生,并为我介绍了职业治疗师和治疗方案,立即开始早期干预。

"进行早期干预类似于上幼儿园,我们需要每天送迪伦去到治疗中心。对于我的家庭而言,这绝对是正确的决定。我们花了很多精力,但治疗开始的时间越早,父母未来的压力就越小。在那里我们能够使用很多资源,老师们也非常耐心。

"多年以来,帮助我儿子的无疑就是教练了,当然不只在专业方面。迪伦总是模仿大他四岁的姐姐。我认为这相当于一路上一直有人在帮他提升运动技能,也就是一对一的教学,个性化援助。总之,有人向他展示或提醒他什么是正确的事情,

并能及时给出反馈就能纠正他的行为。"

特别是从小学到中学,与特殊教育指导李老师的结对,对他的发展至关重要。

这种连续性使迪伦得到了保障,并建立了牢固的师生关系。"她一直与我保持联系,总能想出新东西去尝试和改变。在这个意义上来说,这是真正的个性化定制。毫无疑问,是这种个性化服务改变了迪伦的生活。连续不断的支持系统甚至允许他参加特殊教育机构外的课堂,这对我们来说无疑是个壮举。"

随着学期临近,迪伦即将成为六年级学生,他的母亲却做出了一个重大决定:让他留级一年。迪伦已经完成了所有 IEP(个别化教育计划)的课程,并准备小学毕业。然而,桑德斯夫人注意到迪伦在数学上落后了一年,在语言艺术上落后了将近两年。

"我对校方说:'重读五年级能让他有机会弥补课程的不足,难道不应该让他重读吗?'起初,校方管理人员在犹豫,但我回答说:'我从没找过律师,一直配合你们工作。这次请听我说,班里的孩子在社交方面落后一年,这能让迪伦很好地理解上课内容。'为了儿子,我坚持自己的意见。如果迪伦明年就进入中学,很可能无法应对中学的压力和课业量。"

次年,迪伦上了正规班级的课程,但总是很难保持正确的行为。李老师意识到这个问题后,用冰棍棒为迪伦建立了提醒系统。每当迪伦"行为出错时",李老师就会放一根冰棍棒到

迪伦

玻璃瓶中。当瓶中满三根棒时，迪伦就不得不花更多的时间回到特殊教育学校，"他不想这样做"。所以，这个策略很有效：会激发迪伦去检查自己的行为。

"一位好老师能够在制定必要纪律的同时，帮助孩子学习。在这方面，李老师大概是最棒的。她发现迪伦会花很多时间上厕所，以此逃避课堂，因此李老师对我说：'听起来可能有些残酷，但接下来我只给他七次超时的机会。'我反问道：'七次？'她回答说：'相信我，一旦我给他记超时，他就会被提醒出来上课。别担心，我不会进卫生间的。'连续且个性化的教育系统是非常关键的。"

虽然李老师可以提供连续的支持系统，但她并不适合做朋友。马库斯是一位很受欢迎的同学，午餐时他愿意跟迪伦一起坐，相当于充当了朋友的角色。

"到目前为止，马库斯仍然会和我儿子说话。拥有这个角色榜样并感觉被社会接受是非常重要的，这表示他不是总和特殊孩子待在一起，而是真正感觉到自己在过'正常的生活'。"

总的来说，迪伦的生活没有太多的社交。唯一的朋友是通过社区服务交到的。通过参加一日游俱乐部，他有机会认识新朋友。还会在校园剧中为灯光组提供协助。做志愿者让他处于人群中，其他人会被迪伦的纯真与积极所吸引。因为他的帖子充满善意，人们在 Facebook 中加迪伦为好友。

随着维系友谊变得不那么重要，迪伦开始把目光投向大学。母亲因迪伦开始寻求更多的独立而感到自豪，并且认为儿子如果想上大学的话，就应该让他去。然而，迪伦的父亲却希望他能一直留在家里直到 21 岁。

"他担心如果迪伦此时在大学失败的话，将不会再有任何适合他的活动。但我跟他说：'你要明白，迪伦在学校一直表现很好，如果他想去，就应该让他去。'为了尽可能确保迪伦在大学能度过最好的时光，我聘请了一位女士，她刚刚成立自己的公司，致力于帮助高中生顺利过渡到大学。她会花大半年的时间游走各个大学，了解他们的系所，和学生交谈，了解学校为学生提供支持的方式。因此，我们需要先见这位女士，她再出面和迪伦学校的老师去谈，了解迪伦成功学习所需的环境。她还发现一所不把 SAT（学术能力评估测试，俗称"美国高考"）作为招生程序的学校，毕竟这类考试对迪伦来说真的很困难。"

之后，迪伦需要选择自己的专业。他列了一个兴趣表，最后缩小到酒店服务专业，因为他"一直对酒店如何让客人感到宾至如归很感兴趣"。申请了十所大学，最终被缅因州的一所小型学校录取，进入他们一年的预科项目。该学校面向需要提供额外学术帮助的学生，让他们有机会攻读学位。

"迪伦所在的项目大约有三十名学生。这里有宵禁、自习室，因为年底的目标是做到完全独立，所以只要学生们表现足

迪伦

够好就能摆脱这些制度的限制。从好的方面来说，学校提供了多层次的支持，有一栋专门用于辅导的大楼，教授可以提供支持。从不好的方面来说，随着支持水平提高，我们需要支付更多的费用。"

对迪伦来说，帮他解释作业、让他专注于任务的服务，使他成长为非常有竞争力的学生。事实上，迪伦已经完成了大部分学业要求，不仅可以提前一个学期毕业，而且是以优等成绩毕业。毕业典礼上，桑德斯女士说到，十分感谢该项目对迪伦的付出。

"使迪伦从高中到大学顺利过渡的真正原因是，首先他对学校各种活动的积极参与。他能够与各种与他不同的人接触，非常忙碌。从戏剧社到酒店俱乐部，他无一不尝试。第二，他喜欢独立和学校的支持。每当从学校回到家，他讲话的清晰度和自信程度都非常棒。但是，和我们住的时间越长越没有什么帮助，反而开始丢掉很多东西。最后，由于迪伦不喜欢生活的不确定性，学校为他制定了紧凑的时间表。"

除了扩展大学里的课外活动，迪伦还在附近的一家酒店担任实习生，尽管做着"糟糕的工作"，但他似乎并不介意。

"大多数人实习时，会试图做一些观察与人交谈。但就我而言，我希望迪伦能多一些好奇心。如果工作人员让他铺床或去拿钥匙，他会因完成任务而很高兴。我问他：'你知道前台经理的

职责是什么吗？'他回答：'不知道。'"

事实证明，凯悦酒店提供给迪伦的培训项目非常有价值。经面试之后，迪伦拿到录用函，然后被派参加"疯狂工作90天"。从制作长岛冰茶、前台工作，到制作咖啡和拿铁，他学到了很多技能。当客人午夜叫客房服务时，迪伦是负责接单、制作并送餐的员工。可惜，因为无法通过辨别客人是否醉酒的测试，迪伦没有拿到全职职位。

"此次经历让迪伦学到了，需要帮助时，不应害怕向他人求助。告诉其他人自己是自闭症患者以及这对自己来说意味着什么，都是可以的。只要解释清楚自闭症意味着，你在明白工作内容的前提下，会做得非常好，哪怕需要多一点帮助或理解。如此一来，你就会值得信赖，也会爱上自己的工作。"

此外，迪伦学会了更好地利用工作教练，教练主要负责寻找当地公司来"培训迪伦并提供工作机会"。通过他们的合作，迪伦正在通过 OVR（Occupational Vocational Rehabilitation，职业康复训练）工作，这是一个政府机构，借助该机构迪伦在假日酒店接受了更多培训，但其间的工作是无偿的，所以 OVR 会为迪伦提供资助。

自从大学毕业以来，迪伦参加过多个暑期实习，例如，在多尼公园做保管员。令家人感到吃惊的是，迪伦从来没有抱怨过工作的不悦，哪怕是在炎热的天气倒垃圾或者打扫厕所。

迪伦

"令他如此热心的原因是可以帮助别人。使人们微笑，指导陌生人正确使用游乐设施，之后再打扫卫生都能让他感到被认可。老板在了解他的自闭症之后，时常鼓励迪伦，这让迪伦倍感愉悦。有些时候，迪伦会回到家，嘴唇嘟囔着，自言自语。老毛病会重现出来。作为母亲，及时察觉迪伦什么时候有压力，什么时候需要休息非常重要。不过总的来说，公司还是很喜欢迪伦的，因为他的工作让人非常满意。"

目前，迪伦和父亲住在一起，他自己在地下室生活得非常舒服。有浴室、厨房、客厅，这样的空间给了迪伦一种责任感，并且像是给了他一个更加独立的生活模式，这是迪伦的终极目标。

"关于迪伦的未来，我们探讨过很多次，迪伦也表示他想搬出去住，找一个室友，一起分享账单。作为父母，这对我们十分重要。当迪伦对未来感到紧张或焦虑时，我们告诉他：'你所经历的煎熬并不是只有自闭症患者才会遇到的。每个人都会遇到困难，并且需要在困难中前进，这就是心理素质。'"

桑德斯夫人回顾了她儿子迪伦的自闭症之路，她说："我不知道未来会是什么样。毕竟，其实我从来没敢想过让儿子去上大学、工作之类的事情，只想着好好地爱我们患有自闭症的孩子，然后一直在忧虑中生活。因为，老实说，我一直是惊喜不断。"

*Navigating Transitions*
风雨同舟

# Matt

Lost. Unsure. Surprised. Mrs. Waldorf was overwhelmed when she learned of her son's autism. She had never been exposed to the classification and was taken aback by how her "lively and loquacious" son could be labeled as "impaired in interaction and communication."

"I was at a lack of words because before, you couldn't even catch him," Mrs. Waldorf recalls. "It was to the point that the doctors were amazed at some of the things he did, such as talking and reading. I remember nights when we would sit on his bed, and he would read tall tales to me from this anthology. He would act out the sounds of the characters, imitating the ribbits of the frogs and the clucks of the chickens. And I would sit there beside my son, thinking he's reading to me, and he's not even two yet. Unfortunately, Matt lost his

Matt

interest in reading, and I started to notice that there was an acute difference in his personality when he started regressing at the age of two."

"For example, we had a garden and Matt had always been into gardening. Every time we went out to the backyard, I could never do anything without him coming and grabbing the shovel and correcting me. Like 'Don't do it that way!' Or, if I were picking something, he would say, 'No, mom, you have to pick it this way!' "

"Then, one day, he went out the garden and just sat down and watched me. And that to me was a sign that something was wrong. I even asked him, 'Is something wrong? Where are your words?' and he just sat there. That was a moment that made me go why isn't he talking? Before, when we were out there, he would always talk to me incessantly, but this time, he just sat in the dirt next to me, not correcting me when I held the shovel wrong, or when I picked the tomatoes wrong. That was the kind of moment that made me say to my husband, 'There's something going on.' "

More hints of Matt's disability surfaced over time. He developed habits such as organizing his toys by color and

making sure that different foods on his dinner plate didn't touch. He stopped talking and started moaning whenever he wanted to call his mother. He stopped reading. He stopped smiling. And he even stopped laughing as much.

Mrs. Waldorf had even to put Matt on a leash. "If we turned away for even two seconds, he would be gone, and when we were in public, people would question my parenting. But I would respond, 'It's more important to have my child on a leash and safe, than it is for you not to judge us.'"

Several variables could have prompted this change, such as the introduction of Matt's younger brother Samuel into the family, but like neurosurgeons, Mrs. Waldorf believes "certain parts of Matt's brain didn't mature. His brain released a chemical, so it stopped receiving messages as it was before." In this regard, Matt's change parallels the calcification that happens to senior citizens when they lapse into Alzheimer's, as patterns of thought became scattered and disjointed.

After Matt's diagnosis, his parents agreed to send him to a nearby academy, the Beckett School, where individual learning was specialized for toddlers. There, Matt benefited from limited class sizes and strong guidance from therapists and

Matt

aides. "It was definitely a trial-and-error process," however. In the beginning, for example, Matt was placed in the severely autistic classrooms.

"He was there for six months," Mrs. Waldorf explains, "And I kept imploring the school to transfer him to a different class. I said, 'Matt knows how to talk and read. So just stop going one letter at a time. It is condescending towards him.' The staff, who was skeptical, of course, thought I was in denial."

"I guess one day Matt just got sick of being restricted, so when his instructor was teaching him the letter L, he popped up from his seat and said, "a, b, c, d, e, f, g, h, i, j, k," and recited the entire alphabet. Watching him from the back of the class, I couldn't help but exchange this goofy look with my son; after all, I had known that he understood what he was taught and just needed to find the time to release his potential. Admittedly, it was hard to witness Matt struggle, but it was in my best interest as a parent to nurture him with patience."

Following Matt's demonstration, the school administered an individualized education program (IEP) evaluation for Matt. He was given a series of objective tests to determine the

proficiency of his speech and comprehension and from the data collected, the evaluator constructed a thorough education plan for him. As a result, Matt moved to a multi-disability classroom his following year at Beckett.

"Matt still received speech therapy, but after transferring to the new class where the students did talk, he started communicating better. To my surprise, it was not his inability to adapt that curbed his learning, but his learning environment. The IEP played a critical role in realizing his abilities. By observing his peers in the higher level classrooms, he adopted their behaviors and soon graduated. From there on out, we integrated Matt back into the school district."

"Matt did well in school, but on some occasions, he was incredibly stubborn, which could have been attributed to his autism. One day, his teacher assigned him a project to make lemonade three different ways in science class. At the time, we had two doors to enter the kitchen, and Matt refused to go through the door on the left, because apparently 'the door on the right was good enough.' So, we were having a discussion about the lemonade, because he said, 'I put the powder in the blender, I mix it up, and that's it!' and I responded,

Matt

'No, there are other ways to make lemonade.' But Matt was adamant that there was absolutely no other way to make lemonade. He raged, 'There's only one way that lemonade is made! This assignment is stupid, and I'm not going to do it!'. I soothed, 'You have to understand there are other ways to think. Just like you can come in through the right door, you can enter through the left door as well. Walk with me Matt and let's go through the left door.' Matt flipped out. He fell on the floor and started screaming. Fortunately, in the end, with some guidance, he made his lemonade and went through the left door."

At the school district, Matt was assigned to a self-contained classroom, similar to the multi-disability classes at Beckett. Both included a select group of students on the autism spectrum who were taught by specially trained teachers and who encouraged Matt to explore his interests. Matt's passion for math and science budded at the elementary school.

On the threshold of adolescence, Matt was intrigued by the extracurricular activities offered by his school. Among the list of clubs and sports, Matt displayed a propensity for wrestling.

"At first, I was incredulous," Mrs. Waldorf laughs, "I said,

'really?' But we never kept him from doing anything that he wanted to do. Once he made the team, the other wrestlers treated him like a brother, and up until he graduated, this coterie of boys made sure he was treated well."

While Matt was social around members of the wrestling team, he still struggled to engage with other students at the school. He started "crushing on girls and was hesitant to approach them." As more of his friends on the wrestling team found dates, he became self-conscious of his quirky behavior, contending with feelings of doubt and inadequacy. He thought no girl would ever notice him. To aggravate the situation, Matt was also under a lot of pressure from his counselors to plan his future. Problems that other students handled were impossible for him to manage.

"Matt was in his own world, and I was always worried about his detachment. But I learned to see things from his perspective, which definitely helped. I remember going into his room one day and saying to him, 'Matt, from the time you were young, we gardened. I don't even like getting my nails dirty, but I'm still digging in the dirt, trying to connect with you.' He laughed at the time and said, 'Yeah mom, that's

Matt

funny.' I told him, I know that you can't tell me everything that's going on in your life, but I want you to find someone who can.' Afterward, we agreed to seek a counselor."

Matt's counselor played a pivotal role, to help him gain self-confidence and allay his fears. With the additional aid of his IEP team-his case worker, learning consultant, social worker and school psychologist-Matt matured.

His case worker Mrs. Carter, in particular, had a profound impact on his life.

"When he was in school, Matt would always wear his bicycle helmet around all day long because it didn't fit into his locker. Naturally, the teachers complained that it was causing a distraction in class and diverting the attention of a lot of the other kids."

The following week, school principal Mr. Hamilton called Matt into his office to request him stop wearing his helmet. Matt wouldn't acquiesce to Mr. Hamilton's wishes; he thought if he left the helmet on the bike, it would be stolen.

"They must have spent an hour discussing potential solutions. That's when Mrs. Carter realized the problem, and you know what she did? She bought Matt a wig stand and put

Matt's helmet on it. When Matt walked into school the next day, he pointed to the white mannequin head and asked Mrs. Carter, 'What's this?' She told him, 'This is Matt's helmet stand. Every day now, you can put your helmet here before you go to class and take it off when you leave for him. And it's just for you.' Matt's face lit up, and he hugged Mrs. Carter and said, 'That was so nice of you!'

"Mrs. Carter made a difference in Matt's life by advocating for him. When Matt was a freshman, for instance, Mrs. Carter wanted him to put him on a more rigorous academic 'track' for Latin, science, and math because she noticed he excelled in these subjects. Most kids like him were on lower tracks, so her supervisor disapproved of her idea. She said, 'The law says that Matt is supposed to be in the least restrictive environment, which means he's expected to be in a place where he can flourish most according to his abilities.' In the end, her plan was successful, and Matt was scheduled as what I call it-an oddball-a student who takes AP classes in science and math and is in special education classes for English and history. The district had to rearrange the structure of the entire school for him."

Matt

"After his first day in the accelerated learning program for math and science, Matt came back home and said to me, 'I think I liked it.' It turns out, the other super smart kids were sort of like him too, reserved and focused on academics. He remained in the classes up until his high school graduation."

As the end of junior year dawned, Matt flourished from the continued support from his family and his IEP group. Not only had he secured adequate grades and showed interest in attending a nearby university, but he also found a girlfriend who shared his passion for the sciences. "She didn't mind that Matt was on the spectrum because she was able to look past Matt's impairment and connect with his interests, and above all, his personality."

Mrs. Waldorf observes a photo on her office wall of the couple at prom. In it, Matt, donned in an elegant suit, slips a vivid corsage onto his girlfriend's wrist. Matt's glowing face and his date's dress, emblazoned with jewels, billowing in the wind, capture the moment's excitement.

By the end of high school, Matt decided to pursue a degree at Ridgeville University. The transition, Ms. Waldorf admits, was difficult. "Academically he was absolutely able to do it,

but socially, and in terms of being organized, there was no way Matt could have handled such a high level of responsibility. So, when he got to college, he had suddenly had to learn to wash his clothes, stay on schedule, eat breakfast, lunch, and dinner, plan out all his classes, complete all his homework, finish his labs, and even purchase textbooks. When he came home for Christmas after the semester, he was not the happy camper he once was. My husband and I talked to Matt and offered him a few options: he could come back home, or we could work together to identify some of his weakness and offer suggestions to help him. A week went by, and he said to us, 'I'm going to give it another try.' He went back to college, feeling burdened, and fell into depression."

"After dropping out of university, Matt stayed at home with us. I suggested that he try out some other colleges nearby, but he wasn't interested. At Ridgeville, he had consistently received low marks-C's, D's and even an F in one course-that he was traumatized. He couldn't handle the pressure, so he said to me, 'Is it OK if I just take two classes at a time?'"

After a hiatus, Matt enrolled in community college. There, he benefited from modified course load and received additional

Matt

assistance since he was eligible for academic support. His stress was lowered by accommodations such as being able to take exams in a different classroom with a proctor and receiving extensions on complex assignments.

With less pressure and more time to complete work, he was able to obtain an associate's degree.

While still at college, Matt was eager to find a job. Again, due to his inexperience, Matt struggled. "People with autism usually prefer to be independent, so it took a while for Matt to realize that it was OK to ask for help. He came up to me and said, 'How do you write a resume?' Working together, we applied to most of the businesses in our town shopping complex."

Unfortunately, Matt did not receive many follow-up interviews with the companies because his college schedule limited his availability. However, he made the initiative to contact the disability department at Walmart to express his interests and was called back for an interview. Now, he works as a cashier at the company full-time.

Reflecting upon her son's development, Mrs. Waldorf remembers a significant time in which Matt displayed

incredible affection and care.

"Last year, I had to undergo brain surgery because this liquid CSF, cranial, spinal fluid, was leaking out of my ears. It was causing me to have seizures and making me pass out occasionally. Matt knew that I was going through an operation, but I told my husband not to tell him how bad my condition was. But to make sure that he wouldn't get too worried, my husband still told Matt about the severity of my operation, because usually, I would be running around the house but for that time being, I was ordered to stay in bed. According to my husband, Matt didn't appear to be listening when he told him the news. And that's what Matt does-he doesn't show others what he's thinking. When they arrived home after school, Matt jumped off the truck, without grabbing any of his stuff and ran upstairs to my room. He said, 'Mom, why didn't you tell me?' I said, 'I didn't want to distract you from your school work, honey.' But he responded, 'What if you had died?'

'Then we wouldn't be having this conversation,' I joked. Matt exclaimed, 'Don't say that! Don't talk like that.' After, he got his backpack from the trunk and headed to my mother's room and said to her, 'You can go now. I'm going to take care

Matt

of mom.' His grandmother protested at first, but Matt asserted, 'Nope. Dad said that when he's not here, I'm supposed to be in charge and take care of mom. Even though dad is here at night, he's not going to be here during the day.' I didn't hear their conversation, but that afternoon, my mother packed her things and left."

"Until my recovery, Matt would sit in the rocking chair next to my bed and take care of me. In fact, he even set up a doorbell that I would ring whenever I needed assistance. He put it down on my nightstand and made sure to test the batteries every morning to make sure they would work for me. Every time I would go to sleep, he would always be by my side, wanting to help me, asking 'Mom, want me to make you a shake?' Since I was drinking protein shakes because I couldn't really eat at that time. Some mornings, I would wake up, and the shake would already be there, and he would say to me, 'Mom, it's time for breakfast, and I'm going to sit here to make sure you finish your meal.' The good part of the whole experience was that we had many deep conversations. He would be sitting there, and he'd ask me how I was doing, and I would ask him, 'How was the last semester for you?' and

we would just start talking, touching upon some deeper issues along the way."

Ultimately, what marked Matt's transition into adulthood was not his graduating nor his going to college and getting a job. It was that he was finally able to reciprocate the care and patience that his mother once showed for him.

# 马特

当沃道夫太太知道儿子有自闭症时,她感到迷惑,不知所措,惊讶。这只是她众多感受中的一部分。在此之前,她从未对此有过接触,而且对她活泼爱说的儿子会被鉴定为有互通及交流障碍而感到吃惊。

"我无言以答,因为在此之前你根本追不上他。" 沃道夫太太回忆道,"在某种程度上医生对他所做的一些事情表示惊异,例如说话和阅读。我记得在晚上我们坐在床上,他会从这本选集中给我念神话故事。他模仿角色发声,发出青蛙呱呱的叫声和小鸡叽叽声。我会坐在儿子身边,想着他在给我念书,并且他还不到2岁。不幸的是,马特失去对念书的兴趣,我开始注意到他在两岁时开始退步,个性上有重大变化。

"例如,我们有个花园并且马特总是待在花园里。每次我们去后院,我什么事情都不能完成。他总是走过来,抓住铲子并且纠正我。像'别这样做'!或者,如果我摘些东西,他就说:

*Navigating Transitions*
风雨同舟

'不,妈妈,你要这样做!'

"后来,有一天,他来到花园并且坐在那儿看着我。这对我来说肯定有些不对劲儿。我甚至问他:'有不对劲儿的事吗?怎么不说话了?'而他只是坐在那里。正是此时让我想他为什么不说话了?从前,当我们在外面的花园,他总是不停地和我说话,但这次他只是坐在土地上挨着我,当我拿铲子或摘西红柿不对时,他也不纠正我。正是那种时刻让我对我先生说:'有事发生了。'"

随着时间的推移,马特更多的障碍线索显现出来。他有了新的习惯,例如按颜色整理他的玩具,还有确保在晚餐盘子上不同的食物互不接触。他不说话了,取而代之的是开始发出呜咽声。他不念书了,不微笑了。甚至也不像以前笑的那么多了。

一度,沃道夫太太甚至用皮带拴着马特。我们只是转过身体2秒钟,他就不见了。在公共场合,人们会对我们对孩子的养育发生质疑。但我会回应:"我孩子拴着皮带并且很安全,那么你们就不要评判我们了。"

许多因素都会引发马特如此改变,例如马特弟弟撒母尔的出生,但是就像脑神经医学,沃道夫太太认为:"马特大脑的某些部分没有发育成熟。某些化学物质改变了他脑子的化学成分,促使它不再像以前一样接受信息。马特的变化可以类似为老年人得了老年痴呆时的脑部钙化,思维方式变得分散和不连接。"

马特

马特被确诊后,他的父母同意送他去附近的私立学校,贝克特学校,在那里有专门的幼儿个体化学习。在那里,马特受益于有限的课堂人数和来自治疗助理的强有力的指导。"这的确是一个实验的过程。"例如,在刚开始马特被分配到重度自闭症班。

"他在那儿待了6个月,"沃道夫太太解释道,"而我一直恳请学校把他转到别的班。我说:'马特知道如何说话和写作,所以不要一次只教一个字母,这对他来说是屈尊俯就了。'工作人员当然持怀疑态度,认为我是在逃避。"

"我想有一天马特对受到的限制感到厌烦了,所以当老师在教他字母时,他从椅子上突然站起来并说道'a,b,c,d,e,f,g,h,i,j,k,'并且背出了整个字母表。我坐在教室的后面无能为力地看着他,但是我和儿子交换了一个滑稽的表情;毕竟,我已经知道他知道那些所教的内容并且争取找机会来表现他的潜力。应当承认,见证马特的挣扎是难以忍受的,但是耐心地哺育他的成长是我作为父母应尽的责任。"

他的潜力被意外发现之后,学校管理一个 IEP 项目,即一个个性化的教育项目。他们给马特一系列的客观测试来决定他对语言和理解力的精通熟练程度。从收集的数据,评估者能够建立一套完整的和根据马特的需要的交易计划。据此评估结果,马特在贝克特学校的第二年转入多重障碍班级。

"马特仍旧接受语言治疗,但是他去了新的班级,在那里孩子们说话,他也开始说了。使我吃惊的是不是他没有能力去适应进而阻止他学习,而事实是,他的学习环境阻碍他的发展。因此,IEP在认知他的能力方面起决定性作用。可幸的是,他观察他的同学,他会采纳他们的行为并且不久他就从这个项目中毕业。从那以后,我们让马特回学区上学。

"马特在学校表现良好,但有时他会不可思议地固执,这可能和他的自闭症有关。有一天,科学老师布置用三种不同的方法做柠檬水。那时,我们有两个通向厨房的门,而马特拒绝走左边的门。因为显而易见地,右边的门已经足够用了。当我们讨论柠檬水时,因为他说:'我把粉末放入搅拌机,我把它们混在一起,就是这样。'我回答说:'还有别的方法制作柠檬水。'但是马特固执地认为没有其他做柠檬水的方法。他愤怒地说:'只有一种方法做柠檬水!这是一个愚蠢做法,我不做了!'我平静地对他说:'你要明白还有其他思考方法,就像你可以从右边门通过,同样你也可以从左边门来到厨房一样。马特,我们一起穿过左门去厨房。'这之后,他勃然大怒,他跌倒在地上并开始大叫。值得庆幸的是,最终,他做成了柠檬水并且也从左边门穿行。"

马特被分配所在的学区班级和贝克特学校的多重障碍班级相似;都是由一批自闭症学生组成并且由经过特殊训练的老师

马特

授课。他们都鼓励马特探索自己的兴趣，特别是在小学，马特对数学和科学的爱好萌芽了。

在青春期开始，他对学校提供的课外活动发生兴趣。在俱乐部和体育一览表中，马特更喜欢摔跤。"最初，我对此表示怀疑。"沃道夫太太笑着，"我说：'真的？'但我们从不阻止他要做的事情。他被选入摔跤队后，直到毕业，其他队员对待他像兄弟一般，这群男孩确保马特受到良好的对待。"

虽然马特和摔跤队的伙伴快乐相处，他和其他同学相处仍有难度。他开始像个女孩，他犹豫如何接近他们并且更加意识到自己的古怪行为。随着摔跤队朋友们找到女朋友，马特不得不和怀疑及不适应做抗争。最终，由于他欠缺社交技巧，没有一个女孩注意过他。使情况更加恶化的是马特承受了许多来自辅导员方面的压力，他要决定将来做什么。其他孩子也要面对这些问题，但对他而言极其有特殊意义。

在这期间，马特生活在自己的世界。作为父母，毋庸置疑，我总是担心他的超脱。但是我学会了从他的角度看事情，这很有帮助。记得有一天我走进他的房屋并和他说："马特，从你小时候我们就做园艺。我不愿意把我的指甲弄脏，但我还是掘土，努力和你联系在一起。"那时候他笑了并且说："妈妈，真有趣"。我告诉他，我知道你不可能告诉我生活中的每一件事情，但我希望有人能够做到如此。此后，我们同意去找辅导员。

最终，马特的辅导员在帮助他获得自信心和减轻恐惧方面起到了关键性的作用。当然，马特的进步不仅归功于他的辅导员老师，还有整个 IEP 团队，包括社工，学习辅导员，社会福利工作者以及学校的心理医生。

特别是他的社工卡特太太，她对马特的影响意义深远。

"当他在学校时，他总是戴着自行车防护帽，因为他的储物柜不能容纳防护帽。理所当然的，老师们会抱怨这会造成注意力分散而且使其他孩子注意力转移。转个星期，校长汉密尔顿先生把马特叫到办公室，要求他不要戴防护帽。但马特不会听从汉密尔顿先生的要求。他申诉说如果他的防护帽和自行车放在一起，就会被偷窃并且他也找不到别的地方安放它。他们花了一个小时来讨论可能的解决方案。在那时，卡特太太意识到有问题了，你知道她做了什么？她给马特买了一个假发架子并且把马特的安全帽放在上面。马特第二天来上学，他指着白色的模型头问卡特太太：'这是什么？'她告诉他：'这是马特的防护帽架，今后每一天在去教室之前，你可以把防护帽放在这里。当你离开时，从这里取走它。这只是为你而设置的。'马特显出愉悦的神情。他拥抱卡特太太并说：'你太好了！'

"卡特太太真正使马特生活发生变化，默默地扶持马特。例如马特九年级时，卡特太太希望马特上更难的学术系列课程，就像拉丁语，科学和数学，因为她注意到马特在这些课程上表

马特

现优异。许多像他一样的孩子都在上稍低级些的课程系列,所以她的领导没有同意她的主意。她说:'从法律上讲,马特应该在一种最不受约束的环境中,这意味着他应该在一个能够根据他的能力让他茁壮成长的地方。'最终,她的计划成功了。马特被安排的课程对我而言是独特的,他在科学和数学上学习大学预科课程,而在英文和历史课程上,参加特殊教育班。学区为了他而重排整个学校的结构系统。

"在上完科学和数学快班第一天的课程后,马特回到家里并告诉我,'我喜欢它。'结果表明其他超级聪明的孩子和他有些相似之处——在学术上矜持和专注。他直到高中毕业都在这些班级上课。

"卡特太太对马特至关重要。卡特太太去世时,他感到内心空洞,并且哭了整整一个月。"

在 11 年级末,因着他的家庭和 IEP 机构的支持,马特看似更加稳定和生气勃勃。他不仅取得好成绩而且开始对上附近的大学表示兴趣,并且找到了一个和他有着对科学共同兴趣的女友。她不在意马特有自闭症,因为她能够略过马特的缺陷而和他的兴趣相连,更重要的是他的性格。

沃道夫太太看着办公室墙上两个孩子高中舞会的照片。照片中,马特穿着做工讲究的礼服,把鲜艳的小花束戴在女友的手腕上。马特满脸笑容和他的女伴镶着珠宝随风飘起的长裙捕

获这一激动时刻。

高中结束之前，马特决定去里奇维尔大学攻读学位。沃道夫太太承认这个过程是艰难的。"学术上，他绝对胜任，但在社交和组织管理方面，马特不能够胜任如此高的责任度。因为，当他去大学时，他一下要学会洗衣服，按计划做事，吃早餐，午餐和晚餐，计划所有的课程，完成他的作业，做完实验，甚至买书。当学期结束圣诞节回家时，马特不像过去那样高兴。我和先生与马特交谈，并且给他提供了一些选择：他可以回家来，或者我们一起发现他的弱点并提出建议来帮助他。一个星期过去了，他对我们说："我要再试一次。"他回到学校，感到承受难以置信的重任，并且患上了忧郁症。

"从大学辍学后，马特和我们住在家里。我建议他试试附近一些大学，但他不感兴趣。在里奇维尔大学，他得到低的分数-C's, D's, 甚至有一门课程是F——这使他受到很大精神创伤。他不会处理压力，所以他对我说：'我一次只上两门课可以吗？'"

在短期的间断后，马特注册了社区大学。他不仅受益于所有调整的课程负荷，而且还得到额外的辅助。（基于504条款）马特有资格结束学业扶持。自从高中毕业后，马特认为他仍有权利享受针对个人而制订的教育计划的优惠待遇，并且从未寻求过其他资助。当他知道这些服务在他高中毕业后就不再延续，

马特

为了得到 504 条款下持续的支持，马特申请对他进行再测试。显而易见，他在大学承受的压力因为生理障碍而降低。例如，他可以在另一间教室考试并且复杂作业获得延期。

在减压和有更多时间完成作业的情况下，他能够获得大专文凭。

在大学期间，马特渴求找到一份工作。再一次，由于他没有工作经验，马特找工作遇到周折。"患自闭症人群更愿意独立自主，马特在经过一段时间后意识到寻求帮助是 Okay 的。他来到我身边问道：'你是如何写简历的？'我们一起申请了大多数坐落在本镇的综合购物商家。"

可惜的是，由于大学课程时间安排限制了他的许多选择可能性。马特没有收到多少二次面试机会。尽管如此，他主动联系沃尔玛残疾部表达了他的意愿，并有了再次面试的机会。现在他是这个公司的全职收银员。

回忆儿子的发展，沃道夫 太太记得一个重大的时刻，其间马特表现出令人难以置信的情感和关心。

"去年，我不得不接受一次脑部手术；我的颅骨上有两个洞，因此脑脊髓液从脑子通过耳朵流出。这引发了癫痫和有时使我晕倒。马特知道我要做手术，但我告诉先生不要告诉马特我的情况有多糟糕。为了确保他不是太担心，我先生还是告诉马特我的手术严重程度。因为一般情况下，我会在房子里跑来跑去，

但是那时，我被要求卧床。据我先生所说，当马特被告知这个消息，他好像没有听。马特就是这样——他不表现出他在想什么。他们从学校回到家里，马特从卡车跳下来，没有拿任何东西就跑到我的房间。他说：'妈妈，你为什么不告诉我？'我说：'我不愿意让你在学习上分心。'但他回应：'要是你死了怎么办？''那我们就不会有现在的交谈了。'我开玩笑地说。马特惊叫道：'别这样说！'他从卡车上取回书包并走向我妈妈的房间，并对她说：'您可以走了。我来照顾妈妈。'他的外祖母一开始反对，但马特坚持这样做。'不，爸爸说过，当他不在家，我应该负责并照顾妈妈。虽然爸爸今晚在家，但白天他不会在家。'我没有听到他们的谈话，但是那天下午，我妈妈收拾她的东西回家了。

"直到我恢复，马特都坐在摇椅上照顾我。事实上，他设置了一个门铃，这样我任何时间需要帮助时，按铃即可。他把它放在我的床头柜上并且每天测试电池以确保它工作。我每次睡觉时，他都在我身边，想帮助我，问：'妈妈，要喝奶昔吗？'我因为不能吃饭，一直在喝蛋白奶昔。有时早晨我醒来，蛋白奶昔已经放在那里，他会对我说：'妈妈，该吃早饭了。我会坐在这儿来确保你吃完早餐。'在这个过程中，好的是我们聊得很深。他会坐在那里，并且问我如何，而我则会问他'你上学期如何？'我们开始交谈，聊到一些很深的问题。"

归根结底,标志着马特进入成人的过渡阶段不是他从高中毕业,也不是他上大学和找到工作。而是他最终可以把妈妈展示给他的关爱和耐心汇报出来。

# Ashley

"Sure, there were times when I felt like giving up, but seeing Ashley where she is today, gives me the impetus to keep going," Mrs. Pena says about helping her 18-year-old daughter cope with her autism. "All these years of searching for special programs for Ashley, finding therapists, making sure she is safe-well, they were worth it."

Considering Ashley's early diagnosis of autism and the difficulties she's faced living with this impairment, there is no denying that Mrs. Pena's efforts were indeed "worth it."

As a premature baby, Ashley went into respiratory distress immediately following her birth and was admitted to the neonatal intensive care unit (NICU). She spent the next week at the hospital, where she was on pressurized oxygen, CPAP.

Ashley

Throughout her stay, the staff frequently noted Ashley's sensitive behavior. On one occasion, when the nurse lowered Ashley's airflow supply by 1%, Ashley gave out a sharp cry. "Apparently, it takes a full minute for newborns at the NICU to even register a change of 50%," Mrs. Pena says, "The doctors had never observed such an abnormality, so I suspected that maybe something was going on with my daughter."

A month later, Ashley's family moved to Pennsylvania. As other children developed speech and learned to walk, Ashley remained silent and spent most of her days inactive in bed.

It was during this time that Ashley's symptoms of autism manifested. Mrs. Pena recalls, "Ashley's unusual behavior became really noticeable. She liked to observe people, but was often unwilling to interact with them." During Thanksgiving break that year, Mrs. Pena invited her in-laws to stay at their house. "Even though there were two more people in the house, it was almost as if Ashley didn't notice them there; she wouldn't acknowledge them, and it went beyond ignoring. In her mind, they did not exist."

"I was also concerned about Ashley's frequent elopement. For a while, she would always try to run out the door.

*Navigating Transitions*
风雨同舟

Fortunately, between myself and my three other children, we were able to keep her in the house. We warned her of the dangers of running away, but Ashley didn't seem to listen. It wasn't until she ran outside, slipped on the icy driveway and injured both her knees and elbows that she stopped escaping."

After the New Year, Mrs. Pena decided to take Ashley to an audiologist, to determine if her daughter had a hearing disorder. The doctor told the worried parents: "Ashley's hearing is perfectly normal. She can hear well within the ranges of a child her age, but she does not respond to the human voice unless it is shouting at approximately 90 decibels, the equivalent of a power lawn mower. Other noises she responds to, no problem."

The audiologist's diagnosis prompted Mrs. Pena and her husband to visit their pediatrician, who referred them to Dr. Stern, a special needs doctor.

Shortly before she turned three, Ashley visited Dr. Stern.

At the appointment, the doctor pronounced Ashley with autism spectrum disorder, on the borderline between mild and moderate, none other specified. "I was expecting Ashley to come back as autistic just because she is the youngest of four

Ashley

children and she is quite different from her siblings. But even hearing it, I felt like a weight had fallen on me. Like I had been hit by a truck." Mrs. Pena remembers. "We were fortunate to have gotten lots of information from Dr. Stern. She provided us with essential knowledge of where we could get our daughter help. That's how Ashley ended up on Provider 50 and with Project Connect."

The program Provider 50 introduced Ashley to a therapist who worked with her 15 hours a week. As Ashley started attending school, the time was decreased to 10 hours a week then to four hours. Now, Ashley doesn't receive the help anymore, though she is still eligible.

With the aid of a behavioral specialist at Provider 50, Ashley was not only taught living skills-how to brush teeth, make bed, and set the table-but also social skills that motivated her to interact with others. When playing games such as Candy Land, Ashley had to learn to take turns and to wait for players to draw their cards first. "It was a way for her to learn her colors. A way for her to learn how to show respect. A way for her to exercise patience and a way, ultimately, to have fun."

During this time, "I observed Ashley's interests, as any

parent should-her love for board games, swinging, riding in the car, going for walks, as long as no animals were present, and flying on airplanes, as long as the travel was less than three hours. My efforts allowed me to bond with my daughter, doing activities I knew were comfortable for both of us."

Although the staff at Provider 50 were "absolutely wonderful," the administrators were "somewhat of a nightmare." Getting the necessary services for Ashley was direct. Maintaining them was not. "As a for-profit company, Provider had incentive as their priority, which I believe is a conflict. Giving services costs money, so every now and again, they would casually remark, 'Oh, you don't need as many services as you think you do. I'm not sure how this was assigned, maybe they use a Magic 8 Ball.'

"The company would say, 'We had a doctor review Ashley's case,' as justification. Well, this was a 'doctor' who has never actually been in the same room as my daughter and is disagreeing with the doctors who have been in the same room as my daughter and has interacted with her."

Project Connect, the other service Dr. Stern recommended, was a specialized, state-run preschool for toddlers found

Ashley

eligible under the Individuals with Disabilities Education Act (IDEA). After an evaluation, Ashley qualified to receive free and appropriate services. An occupational therapist and a speech therapist personalized a sensory diet to help her stay focused and Ashley took pleasure in activities such as being brushed by a soft surgical brush.

At the school, Ashley also worked on her communication skills through sign language and later, through an app on her iPad, Proloquo2Go.

"Having a conversation with a nonverbal child is very difficult. If Ashley is upset, I can ask her what's wrong or what's bothering her, but I just may not get a response. She might look at me, not being able to explain, or she might signal help using sign language. I wanted to hone my daughter's communication skills through technology and PATAN-the assistant technology people for the Commonwealth of Pennsylvania-was able to support my endeavors."

For two years, Ashley tested out various models of such communication devices and favored the iPad version; after all, with Proloquo2Go, Ashley could convey her thoughts by tapping the application's buttons-each of which reads a

different word or presents a different image. "Once Ashley understood that she could ask for something and get it, she started initiating more communication. For example, Ashley has decided the only beverage she wants to drink is water. So, she knows the sign for water. One time, she was sitting at the table and did the sign for water, and I said, 'Oh! You want some water! I'll get you some.' After I had got her the water, you could see her happiness. Ashley was surprised since she struggled with getting her point across in the past."

"It was a difficult progress teaching Ashley how to sign and use her iPad. For a while, it seemed that Ashley would only have around 20 signs and if you tried to teach her more, she would lose one to gain one. It was almost as if she needed the brain capacity to store more signs. The main techniques the teachers employed were hand-over-hand and modeling. The therapist would say to Ashley, for instance, 'This is a taco.' and would then show my daughter an image of a taco. Plus, I would also physically model the taco to Ashley, which would reinforce the idea. Ultimately, it came down to repeating the images and models in Ashley's mind so that she could reference what she learned for future need."

Ashley

Now, Ashley is fluent in 75 signs and communicates over 100 phrases using her iPad. "Listening to music," "Going on the swing," "Getting her coat," have integrated into her daily vocabulary. Ashley has also focused on manners such as "please" and "thank you."

"It is certainly hard for her," says Ms. Pena, "but she has applied terms such as 'I'm sorry.'"

After Ashley's graduation from Project Connect, Mrs. Pena noticed that "any negative behaviors, such as hitting and ignoring Ashley had before, were reduced" and that caring for her daughter was significantly easier.

For example: "Before Project Connect, I was the only person Ashley interacted with, probably since I fed her. But after Project Connect, she would go up to her oldest sibling and ask her for a hug, or an arm squeeze. And so, the relationship between the siblings kick-started after Project Connect."

Embarking on a new challenge, Ashley started attending public school in the autistic support classrooms soon after.

"Fortunately, our public schools have an autistic support classroom at every level-elementary, middle and high school. As a student, Ashley has matriculated through this program

from the start and will graduate when she is 21."

At school, Ashley was protected from judgment. In public, though, she faced discrimination. Adults cringed away from her. Neighbors labeled her a freak. Having "zero toleration for such nastiness," Ms. Pena upheld: "Ashley should not be ostracized or alienated because of her differences."

"My sour expression really did all the talking. Quickly, the little kids in our apartment complex realized the consequence of their bullying and began to stop. Advocating for your child, even against a gang of teenage boys, is always the right decision. What makes me proud to say, also, is that Ashley's siblings have also been her protectors. So, for the most part, Ashley enjoyed elementary school."

Surprisingly, unlike most of her peers, Ashley made a smooth and "almost effortless" transition to middle school. Her eighth grade brother had been injured the past year, so Ashley frequently accommodated him to school in the mornings and had accustomed herself to the new environment. Once the academic year started again, Ashley was no stranger to the building's narrow hallways and clamoring lockers. In fact, with the support of the district, Ashley was permitted to

visit with her new instructor, Mr. Patterson, months in advance. Mr. Patterson guided Ashley around the classroom, exciting her with the sand table, swing sets, bundles of stationery and her cubby. "Essentially, Ashley equated middle school and Mr. Patterson to fun, and her early introduction certainly helped navigate this transition."

"In addition, Mr. Patterson built a relationship with the children, so they understood that he was not just their teacher, but also their friend. I think his warm attitude welcomed Ashley and throughout middle school, her social skills have improved, whether due to Mr. Patterson's guidance or not."

Mr. Patterson continued to stick by Ashley throughout high school, serving as that 'constant' factor. Part of why Ashley had little trouble transitioning was because her instructor stayed the same; despite changes in settings, Ashley recognized Mr. Patterson as someone she trusted; she became more composed whenever he was around.

Nonetheless, though Ashley could easily adapt to changes in the school's environment, she was stressed when visiting unfamiliar restaurants, shops, and parks. To ease her qualms, and to prevent sudden outbursts, Ms. Pena arranged short

Navigating Transitions
风雨同舟

tours for Ashley to familiarize herself with the new area. In one instance, "before we took our very first plane flight with Ashley, her behavior specialist brought her to the airport a week in advance. As a 'practice run', we went through security and were allowed on a plane so Ashley could see what would happen. Come time for our vacation, we arrived in a slightly bigger airport, but Ashley had no trouble adjusting at all."

According to Ms. Pena, social stories and drawings that show children with autism how to act appropriately, both maintain Ashley's composure and prepare her for new experiences. The colorful doodles capture Ashley's attention and tell her what to expect. "At the dentist's office, the assistant demonstrates to Ashley the step-by-step process of getting her teeth cleaned, similar to a social story. This way, Ashley could see, 'Oh, this isn't going to hurt, and there is nothing to worry about.'"

Ms. Pena has even developed her strategies that improve her daughter's routine. A few years ago, Ms. Pena noticed Ashley's overconsumption of Pop-Tarts-a pastry high in calories-and Halloween candy. As a pre-diabetic, Ashley needed to limit her sugar intake, and Pop-Tarts were restricted.

Ashley

Ms. Pena, still wanting Ashley to taste her favorite foods occasionally, bought Mini, "fun-size" chocolate instead. "Ashley is allowed one a day, and so far she has adhered to this rule. The smaller pieces of candy don't threaten her diet and keep her satisfied as well."

Regarding Ashley's plans for the future, she is already on the waiting list for a group home where she'll be supervised, get a job and work for as many hours as her disability will allow. Her mother, well advised, took the initiative to contact state agencies ( such as the Office of Vocational Rehabilitation ) and organizations such as SAM ( Service Access and Management ) who will help the family finance the program and housing for Ashley. "We'll have help finding employment and making sure that Ashley gets what she needs to be to able to have her own life."

"A lot of parents are unaware of programs such as SAM, and I only learned about them through Ashley's developmental pediatrician. SAM helps parents find funding for their children, and since Ashley qualifies for social security benefits, she gets a certain number of vouchers per year for things that she needs, like an autistic program in the afternoons, respite care, or going

to a special camp over the summer. Such money can come from the government but also from charities like Easter Seals."

"Children in our state, on the autism spectrum, are mostly sound, aided by the government; adults, however, are not, and this is when SAM comes in. It is the parent's duty, then, to bring together the funds you are receiving with groups such as SAM. Unfortunately, the services are not well advertised or known about."

The fact that there exists such a long waiting period shows that there is less supply than demand and "it is increasingly important that parents think ahead of time." Waivers, though selective, alleviate financial burden and decrease caregiver stress significantly. Even if a child with autism is not yet eligible for services, due to age restrictions, parents should apply anyway.

"Don't be afraid to consult your doctors, teachers or therapists with any questions lingering in your mind. I was lucky to have a pediatrician who informed me of programs that have livened Ashely and not everyone is. The sooner you get the information, the better."

As Ashley matures and reaches the threshold of adulthood,

Ashley

she must once again adapt to a new routine. However, backed by her mother's intricate planning and years of careful instruction, Ashley is confident this change will be as smooth as the others.

"She now understands social manners such as 'you need to be quiet in a restaurant.'" That letting loose with a Tarzan yell isn't appropriate. When she was younger, this would make no sense to her; now that she's a little older, it does."

Ashley has even begun to show affection, which her mother considers a "rare expression."

"A few weeks ago, Ashley's therapist taught her how to say 'hug'. The first time she asked me for one-it was a breakthrough. It was a huge moment for us. It gave me the courage to keep going. Part of the problem of being a parent of a child with autism is that you second guess yourself all the time- 'Am I doing the right thing? Is this really helping?' Sometimes you feel as if your child's progress is one step forward, one step back, two steps to the right. It's never straight progress."

"If it's one thing I've learned, it's to enjoy the baby steps toward reaching your child's goals. In the end, they become strides, helping them fit into society and live a better life."

# 阿什莉

"当然,我也曾想过放弃,但看到阿什莉现在的成就,我便有动力继续前进了,"佩纳夫人为了缓解她十八岁的女儿的自闭症时这样说道。"这些年来为阿什莉寻找各种特殊的治疗方案和治疗专家以确保她的安全——所做的这一切都是值得的。"

考虑到阿什莉的自闭症早期诊断以及她面临的这种障碍所面临的困难,不能否认佩纳太太的努力确实是"值得的"。

作为一个早产儿,阿什莉出生后呼吸困难,住进了新生儿重症监护室(NICU)。她在接下来的一周都是在医院度过的,而且接上了呼吸机。

在住院期间,工作人员经常注意到阿什莉的敏感行为。有一次,当护士将阿什莉的气流供应量降低了1%时,Ashley发出了一声尖锐的哭叫。"通常情况下,新生儿需要整整一分钟才能感受到50%的气流供应量变化",佩纳夫人说,"医生从

来没有观察到这种异常,所以我怀疑也许我的女儿身上发生了某些事情。"

一个月后,阿什莉的家人搬到宾夕法尼亚州。随着其他孩子们开始说话并学会走路,阿什莉始终保持沉默,而且大部分时间都在床上不活动。

在这段时间里,阿什莉的自闭症症状开始显现出来。佩纳太太回忆说:"阿什莉的异常行为变得非常明显。她喜欢观察人,但往往不愿意与他们进行互动。"感恩节假期时,佩纳太太邀请她的岳父留在家里度假。"即使房子里还有两个人,阿什莉却好像几乎没有注意到他们一样;她甚至不认为他们是存在的,而不仅仅是忽视。在她的脑海里,他们根本不存在。"

"我也很关心阿什莉经常发生的事情。有一段时间她总是试图跑出门。幸运的是,我和另外三个孩子能够把她留在家里。我们警告她跑出门的危险,但阿什莉似乎没有听。直到她跑到外面,滑倒在结冰的车道上,擦伤了她的膝盖和肘部,她才停止了逃跑。"

新年后,佩纳太太决定带阿什莉去看听觉病矫治专家,以确定她的女儿是否有听力障碍。医生告诉忧心忡忡的父母:"阿什莉的听力是完全正常的。她可以很好地听到她这个年龄段的孩子能听到的声音,但她并不会对人的声音作出回应,除非是90分贝左右相当于割草机。她对于其他噪音的回应也没有问题。"

听觉医生的诊断促使佩纳夫人及其丈夫拜访了他们的儿科医生,他将他们转交给特殊需要医生斯特恩博士。

在阿什莉快三岁的时候她去看了斯特恩医生。

在此次诊断中,医生确诊了阿什莉患有自闭症谱系障碍,程度在轻度和中度之间,没有其他并发症。"我曾怀疑过阿什莉患的是自闭症或待分类的广泛性发展障碍,因为她是四个孩子中最小的,她和她的兄弟姐妹有很大的不同。但即使只是听到这个消息,我已经像是被卡车撞了一下跌倒了,尽管如此,实际上我怀有期待。"佩纳太太回忆道。"我们很幸运得到了斯特恩医生的信息。她向我们提供了我们能够帮助女儿的基本知识。这就是阿什莉参加了 Provider 50 和 Project Connect 的开始。

"Provider 50 计划允许阿什莉有一名治疗师来到她家,与她一起工作,最初每周工作 15 个小时。然后,当阿什莉开始上学时,每周减少到 10 个小时。时间逐渐减少到四个小时,而现在阿什莉已经不再接受这种帮助了,尽管她仍有资格。"

在 Provider 50 的行为专家的帮助下,阿什莉不仅要学习基本的生活技能——如何刷牙,如何收拾床铺,如何摆放桌子——还有促使她与他人互动的社交技能。当玩糖果土地的游戏时,阿什莉必须学习与其他玩家轮流进行,还有等待其他玩家先出牌。"这是她学习颜色的一种方式,一种让她学会如何表现尊重的方式,一种让她变得有耐心的方式,最终才是获得

阿什莉

乐趣。"

在此期间,"我像所有父母都会做的那样观察阿什莉的兴趣,她喜欢棋盘游戏,荡秋千,开车去兜风,在没有动物的情况下出门散步,还有时间少于三个小时的飞行。我努力使我能够和女儿保持联系,做一些让我们都感到舒服的活动。"

虽然 Provider 50 的工作人员十分优秀,但他们的行政人员却无法恭维。为阿什莉提供的必要服务是直接的,而不是通过他们。作为营利性公司,提供者把激励作为首要任务,我认为这是一个冲突。一次次的服务费用,他们却只会随意地说说:"哦,你不需要像你想的一样多的服务。"我不知道这是如何决定的,也许他们使用了 8 号魔术球。

"公司会说:'我们有一个医生负责阿什莉的案子,'作为辩解的理由。的确有这么一名医生,但他从来没有和我女儿在同一个房间里相处,并且不支持那些和我女儿在同一个房间里与她进行过互动的医生。"

斯特恩博士推荐的另一项服务项目——Project Connect 是符合"残疾人教育法"(IDEA)资格的专门的国营幼儿园。在学校评估后,阿什莉有资格获得免费和适当的服务。

在那里,她得到了职业治疗师和言语治疗师的帮助。"他们想出了一些方式,例如通过制定感官食谱来帮助她保持集中精力条理清晰。"阿什莉接受的活动中她最喜欢的是被软手术

刷轻抚。

在学校，阿什莉还通过手语来学习与人沟通，后来还通过iPad 上的一个应用程序 Proloquo2Go 进行学习。

"与不说话的孩子进行对话是非常困难的。如果阿什莉不高兴，我会问她怎么了或有什么困扰她的，但我可能得不到回应。她可能会看着我但无法解释，也可能会用手语来帮助表达。我想通过科技手段锻炼女儿的沟通技巧，而宾夕法尼亚联邦的助理技术人员 PATAN 能够支持我的想法。"

两年来，阿什莉测试了各种不同模式的交流方式，并显示出了使用 iPad 的明显倾向；毕竟使用 Proloquo2Go 时阿什莉可以通过按应用程序的按钮来传达她的想法，每个按钮都指向不同的单词或呈现不同的图像。"一旦阿什莉明白，她可以要求一些东西并且能够得到它，她就会更主动地与人沟通。例如，阿什莉唯一想要喝的饮料就是水，所以她知道了水的标志。有一次，她坐在桌边，她指给我水的标志，我说：'哦！你想要一些水！我去给你倒水。'当她得到了水以后是很高兴的。她自己也感到惊喜，因为她过去经常因为无法表达自己的想法而感到困扰。在这以后，我会经常看到水的标志。"

毫无疑问，教会阿什莉如何进行标记和使用 iPad 是一个艰难的工作。有一段时间阿什莉似乎只能记住二十个左右的标志，如果再学一个新的她就会忘记一个学过的标志。她似乎做不到

阿什莉

使大脑的能力再存储更多的标志。老师所采用的主要技术是手工制作和建模。例如，治疗师会对阿什莉说："这是一个炸玉米饼，"然后向她展示玉米饼的形象。另外，我也会给阿什莉做一个真的玉米饼，这样可以加强她对玉米饼的认识。最终这些重复的图像和模型会留在阿什莉的脑海里，作为她将来所学知识的参考。

现在，阿什莉已经可以熟练使用七十五个标志和 iPad 中的一百个短语以用来沟通。"听音乐"，"荡秋千"，"穿上外套"，这些词组已经成为她的短语库中的基本组成部分。由于阿什莉前期的精力主要集中在学习命令和要求的短语上，现在她开始转向学习类似"请"、"谢谢"这样的礼貌用语上。"这对阿什莉来说无疑是很难的，"佩妮夫人说，"但她已经学会了说'对不起'"。

阿什莉在 Project Connect 的学习结束后，佩妮夫人发现阿什莉之前所有的消极行为包括打击和无视都有减少。照顾阿什莉变得更容易了，因为阿什莉开始与家庭成员沟通了。

例如："在参加 Project Connect 项目之前，我是唯一一个与阿什莉互动的家庭成员，因为我需要喂她吃饭。但是在参加 Project Connect 之后她开始寻找她的姐姐，要一个拥抱或者挽着手。所以阿什莉与兄弟姐妹们的互动是从 Project Connect 项目之后开始的。

不久之后，阿什莉开始面对新的挑战，她开始在公立学校的自闭症支援教室上学。

"幸运的是，我们的公立学校在小学，中学和高中的每一级都有自闭症支持教室。作为一名学生，阿什莉从一开始就通过这个项目入学，然后在21岁时毕业。"

在学校，阿什莉得到了认真的保护。在公众场合，她却遭受着歧视。成年人们远离她，邻居们把她标榜为一个怪胎。佩纳女士对于这种不耻的行为是零容忍的，她坚持："阿什莉不应该因为她的不同寻常而被排斥或疏远。"

"我的强硬表达比其他一切言语都更有效。很快，我们公寓大楼里的小孩子意识到他们欺凌的后果并停止了这种行为。维护你的孩子，哪怕只是面对一群十几岁的男孩也是正确的决定。令我自豪的是，阿什莉的兄弟姐妹也是她的守护者。所以，在大多数情况下，阿什莉喜欢她的小学时光。"

令人惊讶的是，与大多数同龄人不同，阿什莉顺利地，"几乎毫不费力"地过渡到了中学。她八年级的哥哥去年受伤了，所以阿什莉经常送他去学校，这使得她迅速习惯了这个新的环境。一年以后，当秋天新学期开始时，阿什莉对于教学楼里的狭窄走廊和吵闹的更衣室并不陌生。事实上，在该区的支持下，阿什莉甚至被允许在新的指导医生帕特森先生陪同下进行暑期访问。帕特森先生在课堂上指导阿什莉，并用沙盘、秋千套、

文具盒鼓励她。"基本上,阿什莉将中学和帕特森先生等同于趣事,而她对于中学的前期认识肯定有助于推动这一转变。"

"此外,帕特森先生与孩子建立了关系,以便他们了解到他不仅仅是他们的老师,也是他们的朋友。我认为他的温暖态度对阿什莉的整个中学时期帮助很大,她的社交技巧有所改善,无论是否是由于帕特森先生的指导。

"帕特森先生继续指导了阿什莉的高中,作为稳定的因素。阿什莉的过渡时期没遇到太多困难,一部分原因也是因为她的指导老师没有变;尽管环境有所改变,但是帕特森先生是她信任的人物,有他在身边的时候阿什莉会更镇静。"

尽管如此,虽然阿什莉很容易适应学校环境的变化,但她在去到不熟悉的餐馆,商店和公园时仍然很紧张。为了解决她的痛苦,防止她突然爆发,佩纳女士在去一个新地方时都会为阿什莉安排短暂的旅行。例如有一次,在我们第一次乘飞机出行之前,她的行为专家提前一个星期将她带到机场。作为一个"练习",我们过了安检,并被允许上了飞机,所以阿什莉可以看到会发生什么。而当我们度假的时候,我们去的是费城一个稍微大些的机场,阿什莉适应的完全没问题。"

据佩纳女士介绍,关于自闭症儿童应如何行动的故事和图画都能使阿什莉保持镇定,也可以为她的新经历做好准备。五颜六色的涂鸦会吸引阿什莉的注意力,并告诉她应该做什么。

在牙医的办公室，助手向阿什莉展示了她的牙齿清洁的一步一步的过程，类似于一个故事。这样，阿什莉就会知道，"哦，这不会疼，没有什么可担心的。"

除了故事之外，佩纳女士甚至制定了自己的一套方案来改善她女儿的日常生活。几年前，佩纳女士注意到阿什莉吃了太多 Pop-Tarts，一种甜腻的高热量的万圣节糖果。作为一名糖尿病潜在患者，阿什莉被指示限制其糖摄入量，不能再吃 Pop-Tarts。佩纳女士仍然希望阿什莉能偶尔品尝她最喜欢的食物，因此她买了 Mini，一种小巧的巧克力代替。"阿什莉每天都可以吃一个，到目前为止她很适应这条规则。较小的糖果不会影响她的食谱，而且还能让她感到满意。"

关于阿什莉未来的计划，她已经在一个小组家庭的等待名单上了，在那里她将受到监督，得到一份她的障碍所允许的工作。她的母亲善意地主动联系了国家机构，例如职业康复办事处，以及 SAM- 服务访问和管理等组织，帮助家庭支持阿什莉的项目和住宿。"我们将帮助她找到工作，并确保阿什莉得到她自己生活所需要的东西。"

"很多父母都不了解 SAM 等项目，而我也是通过阿什莉的启发儿科医生才了解了这些。SAM 帮助父母为自己的孩子找资金，而且阿什莉有资格获得社会保障福利，因此她每年都会获得一些特定的帮助，例如下午的自闭症计划，临时看护，或去

一个特殊夏令营。这些钱可以来自政府，也可以来自像 Easter Seals 这样的慈善机构。

"我们国家的自闭症儿童帮助体系在政府的帮助下，大都是健全的；然而，成年自闭症患者却不是这样，就在这种情况下，SAM 出现了。父母的责任就是将收到的资金汇集在一起，然后交给 SAM 这样的机构。

"不幸的是，有时候，我认为这些服务没有很好的宣传，知道的人也很少。"

即使阿什莉只有十七岁，而且她已经在好几个项目的等待名单上，但是获得她需要的强制性援助可能需要几年时间。只有提前注册她才会在满 21 岁时被优先考虑。等待时间很长的事实表明现在供少于求，父母提前考虑这些问题越来越重要。有选择地减轻经济负担，减轻照顾者的压力。即使一个自闭症儿童由于年龄限制还没有资格获得服务，父母也应该提前申请。

"不要害怕咨询你的医生、老师或治疗师，你心中有任何疑问都可以询问他们。我很幸运有一名儿科医生告诉了我这个能帮到阿什莉的项目，但不是所有人都会这样做。你获取信息的速度越快越好。"

随着阿什莉逐渐成熟并达到成年的门槛，她必须再次适应新的日常生活。不过，由于她母亲的复杂规划和多年的精心指导，相信阿什莉这一阶段的转变将会像其他人一样顺利。她现在明

Navigating Transitions
风雨同舟

白了社会礼节,比如"你需要在餐厅里安静","像泰山一样大喊大叫是不合适的。" 当她年纪还小的时候她并不明白这些意味着什么,现在她成熟了。

阿什莉甚至开始表现出情感,这在她母亲看来是非常不容易的。几个星期前,阿什莉的治疗师教她如何说"拥抱",这是她第一次问我——这是一个突破。这对我们来说是一个重大的时刻,它让我有勇气继续前进。作为自闭症儿童的父母,一个很重要的问题就是你会反复地质疑自己——"我做的对吗?这真的有帮助吗?""有时你会感觉你的孩子进步了一点,又后退了一点,再进步更多一点。这不是一个直线上升的过程。"

"如果我从中学到了什么,那就是享受你的孩子一点点进步最终实现目标的过程。最终,他们会长大成人,我们会帮助他们融入社会,过上更美好的生活。"

# David

On a brisk summer evening in Orlando, Florida, David and his mother board the monorail back to their hotel at Disney Resorts. Donned in trousers and a loose shirt, the 20-year-old takes a seat on the empty train. His mother sits down beside him.

As the train glides down the rails silently, David looks out at the lake below them-the reflection of hotel lights that illuminate the water and the dark cape of the night shadowing figures.

Suddenly, fireworks rocket from the distant theme park. David's mother looks over at her son, concerned that he would be disconcerted by their noise. After all, as an individual diagnosed with autism, David had always been sensitive to such commotion. At home, he would wince at the roar of thunder and

cry at loud pep rallies, where the chants from the crowd scared him. Inside the train, however, David observes the fireworks' beauty. He watches the light show in awe, his eyes bouncing from one spectacle to another. Each time a firework descends, a new one rockets up. He looks over at the strangers on the bus and exclaims, "This is so beautiful!"

Despite his mental impairment, David had always been very social. This characteristic, rare for individuals with autism, was the reason he had missed his diagnosis for years. Until David moved to Maryland at age 3, no one noticed his disability. Once he entered kindergarten, he was integrated as a part of the regular school curriculum and was known to be welcoming and kind.

David learned from interactions with his peers and emulated their behavior. As he saw how the other kids-ones who didn't need special services as he did-paid attention to class, and how they worked quietly and efficiently, he learned to apply those behaviors.

Still, David struggled to overcome challenges with autism. Aside from his delayed learning, David's hyperactivity and attention deficiency were evidence of his disability. He would

David

throw tantrums when his mother cut his nails, for instance, or when the barber cut his hair. At the dentist's office, in particular, David would fidget in his seat uncontrollably.

Fortunately, to alleviate the situation, David's mother found that her son was consoled by nursery rhymes and friendly conversations with the dentist. David's mother recalls, "We were at the dentist's office, and they had suggested we use anesthesia to soothe David. Personally, I didn't think this was in our best interest. It was funny how we solved the dilemma, though. The doctor ended up speaking to David for the entire hour to keep him entertained." David cooperated during the operation, entertained by the doctor's stories and questions.

The following year, David moved to a different middle school, where the dynamics were different. The district checked the number of classes he could take with non-special education students, so he spent the most time with children on the low-functioning end of the spectrum. Everyone there had greater difficulties communicating and interacting than he did.

"The program did not give much inclusion, so he wasn't given any role models. As David copied other people in the class who were nonverbal and displayed more impulsive habits,

he regressed in behavior significantly." To guide him in a more proper direction, David was assigned a one-to-one mentor who aided him tremendously. "As he grew older, I noticed that David did not just prefer one on one teaching," his mother says, "he needed it. For him, it was critical because as such a flexible learner, he needed to distinguish what was appropriate from what was not."

Evidently, David's adolescent years marked a changing point, as he faced many decisions for his future. "We decided to have a meeting with David and his mentors to discuss his interests and potential schooling in the future." David's mother says, "Of course, David's first choice was to become an engineer. He had always loved trains since he was little. Unfortunately, that was not possible because of his hyperactivity."

Although he had been desensitized to loud noises, David still had trouble directing his attention to the assigned tasks and struggled with multi-faceted problems listing numerous steps. His family decided David should incorporate the design and technology aspect of engineering into his education, but choose a focus that had little mental strain. In the local college,

David

there was a course that accepted special education children and taught them the fundamentals of graphic design. Through a job coach the school district provided, David secured a spot as a part of the incoming class.

David's mother remembers it as a warm fall morning when her son attended his first day at Millbrook Community College. His knapsack, lined with papers, was slung over his right shoulder as he climbed out of his mother's car and leaped onto the pebbles on the sidewalk's edge. A mentor was waiting for him at the end of the pathway.

"As a parent, it was comforting to realize that David could be independent at college with the help of an assistant volunteer. She [the volunteer] was able to facilitate the learning process and helped David by sending us feedback on his progress and breaking down tasks for him when the assignments were more challenging than usual. Programs like the one offered at the school really guided David to become more self-directed. Above all, it helped him integrate with society, as he developed friendships with his classmates and had classwork to complete after school as well."

Aside from pursuing a post-secondary education, David

and his parents also worked with the district's job coach to identify other career opportunities available to David outside of his local college. Initially, David volunteered at the library; his mom shadowed him closely and helped him sort the books alphabetically. Over longer periods of time, however, David's mother realized that her son's hyperactivity limited his focus.

"One moment he would be categorizing a book, but right after, he would be shuffling down the aisle, carrying the cart along with him. Additionally, David would sometimes misplace books; this would cause confusion for library visitors, though they were all very friendly and understanding."

David also pursued another job at the laundromat. Under his state's "Employment First Policy," he enjoyed a fair pay during this stint but, despite his affability and work ethic, David was easily distracted by the bustle of people, who were scurrying in and out of the shop. Once, while David was observing an exchange between his manager and a customer, he poured an entire bottle of detergent in the washing machine.

"His attention-deficiency, along with his fault of hand-eye coordination," his mother remarks, "encouraged us to explore other potential occupations. Looking back, I am

David

grateful we started job sampling early. We were able to try out a wide gamut of jobs from working at the animal shelter to our town's Rite Aid. Ultimately, through the process of elimination, we were able to narrow down our options. As of now, because of his enthusiastic personality, David is interested in a career in customer service and currently a volunteer at Special Olympics Young Athletes, a program that allows him to aid younger children with disabilities.

In large part, Special Olympics "changed David's life." It taught him self-determination; at the beginning of every season, David chooses the sports he wants to play, and as the organization requires, he must learn to dedicate his time to practices and games. It taught him healthy competition; since individuals get to compete at their own skill level at the program, David's self-esteem was boosted by the small victories he had during team activities. It taught him how overcome losing. And it taught him to how to make friendships with others. Ultimately, "Special Olympics has taught David that his autism is what makes him who he is, and that he doesn't need to change to conform to society's standards-to be perceived as normal-and that he goes through life just like

anyone else. His struggle with autism, though perpetual, is just like that of anyone else's."

A train passes by outside, shaking the room slightly. It maneuvers past power lines and dirt roads, onto the horizon.

Looking out the window fancifully, David's mother concludes, "Both my son and I have faced so much on this journey. I'll admit it was rocky at first. But with the help of volunteer programs and the early initiative and willingness to help David transition, there is no doubt in my mind that David is at a new stage of independence in his life now and I am confident that he is equipped with the resources and support to maintain a comfortable lifestyle."

# 大卫

在奥兰多，弗罗里达清风袭人的夏夜，大卫和他的妈妈坐在从迪斯尼乐园回旅馆的单轨车上。穿着宽松的T恤衫，这个20岁的年轻人坐在一辆几乎无人的车厢里，他的妈妈坐在他的旁边。

列车安静地沿着轨道徐徐前行，大卫远看着下面的湖面——旅馆的灯光反射在它上面，人影在黑暗的夜色里晃动。

突然间，烟火从远处的主题公园冲天而起。大卫的妈妈目光转向儿子，担心他会因为这些声音而心烦意乱。无论如何，作为一个被诊断有自闭症的个体，大卫对这种喧哗纷扰一直很敏感。在家里，他会因为轰轰的雷声而畏缩并且从人群中发出的赞美声音会吓到他，让他因赛前动员会而哭泣。然而，在火车里，大卫能够欣赏到美丽的烟火。儿子观赏着烟火，眼睛从一个惊喜跳到另一个惊喜。每一次的烟火引发了新的高潮。他转向列车中的陌生人，欢呼着："这太美丽！"

大卫虽然有精神缺陷，他从小就一直愿意和别人打交道，这一特征是在一般自闭症患者中很少见，也是他多年一直被误诊的原因。直到他3岁搬到马里兰州之前，没有人注意到他的残障。在他进入学前班时，他被分到学校普通课程班，并且以爱说和和蔼著称。

大卫通过和他的同龄人接触学习东西并且模仿他们的行为。大卫观察那些不需要特殊服务的孩子们——他们上课注意力集中，他们如何安静有效的学习，他也把这些应用到自己的生活中。

尽管如此，大卫仍要克服自闭症患者特有的挑战。除了学习滞后，大卫异常地好动和注意力不能集中，这些证实了他的残障。例如，在妈妈给他剪指甲或剪头发时，他会发脾气。特别是在牙医诊所，大卫会毫不顾忌地烦躁。

值得欣慰的是，大卫的妈妈让儿子听摇篮曲以及和医生交谈会缓解许多上述情况。大卫的妈妈回忆道，"在牙医诊所，他们建议用麻醉药来使大卫放松。对我个人而言，不认为这是最好的方案。我们解决这一难题的方法非常有趣。医生最终和大卫聊了整整一个小时来让他高兴。"在治疗过程中，大卫对医生的故事和问题很感兴趣，他全程配合医生的治疗。

接下来一年，大卫去了不同的初中，在那里有许多不同。学区查看了他能够和正常学生一起上的课程，这样他大多数时间都是和那些自理能力较低的孩子们在一起。这些孩子在交流

大卫

和互动方面比大卫更具困难。

  这个方案没有包容性，因此他没有任何榜样。随着大卫模仿那些非言语和更具韧性的习惯，他在行为上有巨大的退步。"为了引导他有一个适宜的方向，学区分配给大卫1对1的老师，这对他有极大的帮助。随着大卫的长大，我注意到大卫不只是更偏爱一对一的学习，"他妈妈说，"他需要这种帮助。对他而言至关重要，因为作为一名灵活的学习者，他需要区分什么是适宜的，什么不是。"

  毋庸置疑，随着大卫面临着许多有关未来的决定，他的青春期标志着转折点。"我们决定和大卫及他的指导老师开一次会，讨论他的兴趣和将来可能的学校。"大卫的妈妈说，"当然，大卫的第一选择是当一名工程师。他从小就喜欢火车。不幸的是，由于他的多动症使它变成不可能。"

  大卫虽然对大的噪音不敏感，他仍然有困难集中精力完成任务并且对多层面、多步骤的问题困惑不前。他的家庭决定大卫未来的学习应包括设计和工程技术方面，但同时挑选一个不需过度脑力劳动的领域学习。在附近的大学，开设一门接受需要特殊教育孩子的课程并且传授他们基本的图形设计。通过学校的工作教练，大卫获得了一个上课的名额。

  大卫的妈妈记得那是在一个暖秋的早晨，他的儿子第一天在米尔布鲁克社区大学上课。他从妈妈车里爬出来，右肩背着

塞着许多纸的背包,欢跳在石子路上,指导教师在路的尽头等待着他。

"作为父母,欣慰地感受到大卫可能在大学期间在助理义工的帮助下独立自主。她(义工)能够协调大卫的学习过程并且通过反馈给我们大卫的进度来帮助他。当作业比平时更具挑战性时,帮助大卫把任务分解。学校提供的类似的安排引导大卫更加自我导向。不仅如此,随着他和同学们发展的友谊以及课后作业的完成,这些都帮助大卫融入社会。

除了接受高等教育之外,大卫和他的父母还和学区的工作指导一起找出社区大学之外的其他工作机会。最开始,大卫在图书馆做义工,他的妈妈紧紧跟随他并且帮助他按字母分类书籍。经过较长一段时间,大卫的妈妈意识到他的多动症使他不能专注。"一会儿,他会把书分类,但马上,他会推着书车跑下走廊。除此之外,大卫有时会把书放错地方。这会使借书人产生怀疑,虽然他们都很友好和善解人意。

这之后大卫决定试试别的工作,这次是在一家洗衣店。按照州政府雇员第一的规定大卫享受着公平的工资支付。尽管他有能力和职业道德但洗衣店匆匆过往的人们会经常让大卫不能专注。有一次当大卫看着他的老板给一位顾客找零钱的时候他把一整桶洗衣液倒进了洗衣机。"他不能集中精力和手脚不协调," 他妈妈解释道。"这促使我们去寻找其他可

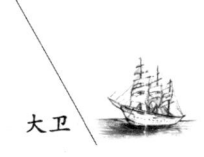

大卫

能的职业。现在回头看我真的很高兴我们在大卫能独立工作的门槛之前就开始了工作尝试。我们尝试了广泛的各种工作,从动物庇护所到我们镇上的瑞得药店。最终通过一系列的筛选,我们能够得到一个很小的选择范围。到现在因为他热情的性格,大卫正在尝试顾客服务这一职业,并且在特殊奥林匹克青少年运动员组织中做义工,这个项目让大卫有机会去帮助有残疾的青少年。"

从大方面讲特殊奥林匹克活动改变了大卫的生活。除了指导青少年,大卫还得到了志愿组织的陪训。这教会了他自我决定。在每一个赛季开始的时候,大卫选择他想要做的体育项目按照组委会的要求,他必须参加训练和比赛。这教给了大卫公平有益的竞争。因为每个人都在各人的水平上竞争,每一次团队活动中的小胜利都大大增加了大卫的自信。这又教会了他如何克服失败如何与同龄人建立友谊。最终特殊奥林匹克活动让大卫知道了自闭症塑造了他,他不需要为此改变来适应社会的标准,要把自己看作正常人一样生活。尽管是长期的,他要努力像其他人一样,他的努力是与自闭症抗争。

一列火车从外面飞驰而过,轻微地震动了屋子、穿过了高压线、跨过了土路、驶向地平线。

看着窗外憧憬着未来,大卫的妈妈最后说:"在这个旅途上我和我的儿子经历了许多。我承认在起初不是一帆风顺,但

在自愿者项目的帮助下和早期参与以及帮助大卫转变的决心中，我毫无疑问地认为大卫已经步入了独立生活的新阶段。并且我相信他有着足够的资源和帮助去过一个舒适的生活。"

# Peter

"Peter, pass me the pink sugar pouch, please," Mrs. Toylas asks her son on a Sunday morning at Perkins Diner.

A 23-year-old rummages through an assortment of colored packets and picks up a white pouch. Before turning to his mom, he hesitates. Then, flipping to the bottom of the pile he hands his mom a pink packet.

Meet Peter, an adult with severe autism.

"Peter wasn't always like this-this well behaved, I mean," Mrs. Toylas explains as she sprinkles the sweetener in her iced tea. "When he was a little guy, he was so horrible and out of control. He dragged his feet and banged his knees until they bled. Peter also used to bite me about 100 times a day. He didn't understand the damage he was causing."

Mrs. Toylas glances at Peter, who sits next to her patiently with a plastic straw dangling from his mouth.

"And I remember when he was 18 months old and in a play group. A lot of the mothers suspected Peter had autism and I began to have suspicions as well. When I took him to a doctor, the professionals thought he was hearing impaired. But six months later, he was diagnosed with autism. The teachers at the play group, who had never dealt with anyone with autism, were really stressed and didn't know how to deal with Peter. He would hit them and run around in circles. He didn't talk, just run. So after having the NJ CAT to evaluate the degree of his autism and determine the extent of his services, Peter was categorized as 'Most Impaired'."

Mrs. Toylas looks back at her frustration.

"As a parent, I was distraught and frustrated. Imagine learning your child feel on the lowest end of the spectrum."

"Before I didn't know how to deal with Peter-he wasn't a regular kid. When we took him to a special needs school, Atan, it was much better. Peter would sometimes bite the teachers and leave scars in their skin-he was very uncooperative at first-but the specialists never complained. He always wanted to do his

Peter

own thing, but he learned to behave. Going to the school really changed our lives."

Peter stays calm beside his mother in the diner's booth, looking out the window. Despite attending a special needs school in the morning, he spends most of the time with his mother at home. And as Peter dips a crispy French fry into some ranch, it's hard to imagine the "horrible and out-of-control" child he was before.

2000

Peter was seven when he escaped from home for the first time. At the time, Peter was left alone in his house, though his father was in their backyard weeding the garden. The gate was unlocked and Peter, unaware of the danger, sauntered past the driveway. He crossed a congested road before settling down at a nearby jungle gym.

When Mr. Toylas went inside to find Peter, no one was home. Moments later, his wife "nearly collapsed," hearing the alarming news from her husband.

"We ran all over the neighborhood," Mrs. Toylas recalls, "I was panicking, and my heart was racing. It was the scariest

Navigating Transitions
风雨同舟

moment of my life." Half an hour later, unnerved and terrified, she found Peter at the playground.

"I remember just collapsing on my neighbor's lawn. I was nearly going to have a heart attack," Mrs. Toylas says. "Both Peter and I have been through a lot."

Throughout that year, Peter would continue wandering around the neighborhood, escalating Mrs. Toylas' anxiety.

2002

On a Tuesday afternoon, Peter had downed so many cans of Snapple that he had a seizure. At the tender age of nine, Peter had a drinking problem, but not the type most people would expect.

"My son had a habit of drinking whatever is in front of him, soda, water, bleach, even T-shirt dye. That day, we had left some cases of Snapple in the garage, and Peter snuck a bunch of them into his room. The fluids messed up his electrolytes, and he started to shake uncontrollably."

Another time, Peter found T-shirt dye during class. Without thought, he snatched the bottle and took a gulp. His frantic teacher alerted poison control immediately. Fortunately,

Peter

Peter was safe, and his mother was assured that the dye had not damaged his health.

2005

At age 12, Peter tended to be apathetic about most activities and didn't pursue any hobbies. On an impromptu trip to Six Flags, however, he fell in love with the park's rickety train ride and a vibrant carousel. He ruminated about the hectic day, unable to fall asleep. Until 3 AM, he chanted, "Six Flags! Six Flags!"

"It was really quirky. I had to stay up the whole night watching Peter, but I just found it really funny. And inside, I felt happy." Mrs. Toylas chuckles.

2006

This was the year when Peter's church underwent construction. A new section, where the Toylas Sunday service would be held, was annexed to the main building. As the family scrambled to attend mass, Peter lingered at the stone doors of the main building.

Mrs. Toylas called out, "Peter! Come here! Come here!"

as she motioned with her hands, "The service is now in this building. We won't be going to that building anymore." But Peter refused to move. He stayed facing the door, with a stone expression.

"He didn't talk, but it was clear that he was confused and wanted to enter the old part of the church. It's tough for people like Peter to adapt to new environments," Mrs. Toylas took a sip of her tea and looked over at Peter, "Sometimes, they just need a little time."

Mrs. Toylas continues to explain how Peter has no desire to have friends, and always misses his sister, who is now in university. She asks her son, "Do you miss Charlotte?" and he nods.

2007

As Mrs. Toylas describes her son's journey with autism, Peter looks down at his fries, nudging her. He is limited in his speech and indulges in the music playing through the diner's speakers instead.

"The first time I took Peter to New York was when he just turned 13. That day, no one could babysit him, so I took him

Peter

out with his sister and his friends," Mrs. Toylas reminiscences.

"My daughter's really into musical theater, so we went to a couple of Broadway musicals. *West Side Story*, *Lion King*, *Trip of Love*, and oh yeah-*Mama Mia*. Peter really enjoyed *Mama Mia*."

Peter scratches his head as if contemplating his favorite show.

Mrs. Toylas explains that Peter was different than other individuals with autism since he can tolerate loud noises. And he is allowed to sit with the general audience during Broadway shows and treated just like everyone else. The staff at the door greet him, hand him a program, and usher him to his seat.

For Peter, the performances are not the highlight of a visit to the city. Rather, it is riding public transportation. On the bus, Peter spectacles at the towering skyscrapers and the bustling streets. At the subway station, he swipes his metro card and bounds through the turnstile. He has ridden the train for an hour, from midtown to Chinatown, watching the world pass.

"He likes the subway because he thinks it's a ride, like one of those at Six Flags," Mrs. Toylas looks over at Peter and grins.

"It's surprising actually. You would expect New Yorkers to be very aggressive and stingy, but when Peter and I went to New York, everyone would lend their seats to Peter. Even the

people buried underneath their sweatshirts with their earbuds plugged in.

The New Yorkers were so generous, especially the people in Times Square. We were waiting for our tickets, and the guy who worked there saw Peter, who was really uncomfortable being squished in the middle of the horde. He called us over and pulled us out of line. Then, he brought us to the front, and we were the first ones to get our tickets!"

"And during the show, a chauffeur offered us disability seats, even though Peter can walk and function. It really goes to show how kind people can be, which is always appreciated."

2008-2014: "People with autism also have impaired imitation skills-one thing they tried to teach him at Atan was to imitate motions like hand clapping. But grasping such physical skills was difficult. That's when we introduced Applied Behavior Analysis teaching methods, which focuses on learning through positive reinforcement. So whenever he successfully imitated his teachers at Atan or even did something right at home, we would reward him. The shift from traditional teaching methods to ABA methods not only helped Peter learn more efficiently but also helped Peter improve his behavior and

Peter

mentality. Something I think all autistic parents should really consider implementing···"

During this time, Mrs. Toylas also realized Peter didn't care what others thought about him. When others would stare at him or comment on his appearance, he didn't mind.

"I think the important thing is that there's a point when you don't care what people think. It's their problem."

2015: Last year, Peter graduated from extended care at Atan Autism Services. At 22 years of age, he had no formal academic education but has maintained a few minor jobs: packaging dog treats, filling mail, and cleaning group homes. And although he struggled academically, Peter was able to acquire simple mechanical skills, such as vacuuming and cooking, by being employed. For a while, he even folded the programs at the Metropolitan Opera.

Despite his basic proficiency, Peter still had a severe case of autism and needed guidance from teachers and therapists. So Mrs. Toylas decided she should fill out an application for Peter to live in a residential home, while receiving all the care he needs, throughout his adulthood.

"The application process to get Peter in a residential

home was very drawn out. I was told that because of the limited spots and the long list of applicants, he wouldn't receive a spot in the home until he was 30. Of course, I wanted him to be in the home immediately, but the residential system revolves around need-based priorities and the individual's degree of impairment. My son is very helpful and obedient, so it really isn't too difficult to take care of him at home." Mrs. Toylas says. "But for other parents, it might be extremely hard to tend to their children."

Mrs. Toylas sighs and starts to rant in frustration, "We really want Peter to reside in a permanent home, though. Also, I know it sounds morbid when I put it like this, but if my husband or I were to die in a car crash tomorrow, we want to make sure that Peter is cared for. We wouldn't want our 18-year-old daughter caring for Peter because she has her whole life to plan out! Anyway, NJ is a very progressive state, but I kind of wish that everything wasn't a giant bureaucracy. Like if I had a problem, I would want the government to be more streamlined if anything else."

Peter nods his head suddenly as if sympathizing with his mother.

Peter

As she watches Peter affectionately, Mrs. Toylas says, "Sometimes I don't think Peter cares about me. I feel like he doesn't really reciprocate my love, but maybe it's just because he doesn't understand. You know, I've been doing this for 25 years, and I'm getting a little tired⋯ like just the other day I was drinking a cup of coffee from Dunkin' Donuts, and he wanted me to pour out my drink just to play with the cup. At times, he'll do something imprudent, and it's as if he doesn't even consider my feelings." She tucks a lace napkin into the collar of his shirt to keep the ranch from staining its navy print.

She concludes, "But at the end of the day, Peter and I, well, we wouldn't want to be anyone else. You know, the other day I asked Peter if he wanted to go to college, like his sister, and he responded, 'No, I want to stay with you.'"

"Even if he knows he's different, he doesn't care. He likes the way he is. He doesn't want to be like his sister, hang out with friends, or go to college and not live with us. People will judge us; they always do. Honestly, though, who cares? Again, it's their problem, not ours. I think we're both happy with the way things are."

Navigating Transitions
风雨同舟

# 皮特

那是一个星期天的早上，在彼林餐厅一个靠窗的餐桌旁，特尔斯夫人对坐在身边的儿子说："沃克，递给我一包粉色的糖袋。"

这个二十三岁的年轻人匆匆地在放有各色糖袋的小筐里找了起来。他拿起了一个白色的糖袋，就在给他妈妈之前，他犹豫了一下，随后又翻了一遍小筐，挑出了一个粉色的，递给了特尔斯夫人。

与皮特的会面开始了。皮特是一个严重自闭症患者。

"皮特不总是这样，我的意思是，不总是表现得这么好。"特尔斯夫人一边把糖撒到冰茶里，一边解释道，"皮特小的时候，很可怕，不能控制自己。他能在地上打滚，击打膝盖，直到流血。他能一天咬我一百次，并且不觉得是在伤害我。"

特尔斯夫人看了看沃克。皮特坐在她旁边，嘴里的吸管晃来晃去。

皮特

"我记得皮特十八个月的时候,那时他在一个幼儿班,很多妈妈,包括我自己,都觉得皮特可能有自闭症。我就带他去看医生。医生开始认为沃克有听力问题,但六个月以后,皮特被诊断为自闭症。"特尔斯夫人接着说。

"幼儿班的老师从来没有和自闭症的孩子打过交道。他们很紧张,不知所措。皮特有时会打他们,然后转着圈子跑。皮特不讲话,就是一个劲地跑。我们给皮特做了新泽西州政府残疾人部门的'新泽西综合评估工具'测试,通过问答,对沃克的评估结果是:严重残疾。"

特尔斯夫人回忆起过去的磨难。

"以前,我们不知道对皮特怎么办,他不是一个正常的孩子。但当我们把他带到一个叫爱顿的特殊学校以后,情况变得好了起来。刚开始,皮特有时咬老师,在老师们的皮肤上留下了疤痕。受过专业训练的老师们从来不抱怨。皮特总是按照自己的想法做事,但是他慢慢开始学会了守规矩。来到特殊学校真是改变了我们的生活。"

皮特平静地坐在妈妈旁边,看着餐厅窗外。尽管皮特上午能上特殊学校,但是大部分时间,他是和妈妈待在家里。看着皮特拿着炸薯条去蘸酱,很难想象他以前是个很可怕,不能控制自己的孩子。

## 2000年

皮特第一次走丢是在他七岁的时候。当时,皮特一个人留在屋里,他爸爸在屋外除杂草,院子里的门没有锁上,皮特不清楚周围的环境,东看西看地就走过了自家的车道,接着走过了一条拥挤的马路,来到了附近的一个儿童公园。

当特尔斯先生回到屋里,他怎么也找不到皮特。过了一会儿,特尔斯夫人回来了,当她得知皮特丢了,她几乎都要崩溃了。

"我们找遍了附近所有地方," 特尔斯夫人回忆起当时的情景说道,"我非常恐慌,心怦怦直跳,这是我一生中最可怕的时刻。"大约半小时以后,特尔斯先生在儿童公园找到了皮特。整个事情至今还让人后怕。

"我记得我当时瘫坐在邻居家的草坪上,我觉得我都快要犯心脏病了。" 特尔斯夫人说,"我和皮特一起经历了很多这样的事。"

那一年,皮特经常在我们小区乱跑,给我们带来了很多麻烦。

## 2002年

在一个星期二的下午,皮特喝了大量的他屯积的斯奈普饮料。在九岁的时候,皮特开始有了喝饮料的问题,这不是人们常说的酗酒问题。

"我儿子有个毛病就是喝任何放在他面前的东西,苏打饮

皮特

料,水,漂白剂,甚至 T 恤衫染色剂,"特尔斯夫人叹了口气说。

"有一天,我们把几箱斯奈普饮料放到了车库,皮特偷偷地搬了一些到他屋里。大量的斯奈普饮料破坏了皮特的电解质平衡,他无法控制地抽动起来。"

还有一次,皮特在教室里看到了一瓶 T 恤衫染色剂,他一时冲动就抓了过来并且打开喝了一口。老师紧急地给有毒物品控制中心打电话。幸好,皮特安然无恙。特尔斯夫人也得到确认那个染色剂对健康无害。

2005 年

从 12 岁那年,皮特开始变得对大多数活动不感兴趣而且他自己也没有什么爱好。但在一次无意中安排的活动里,皮特一下子喜欢上了"六旗世界"游乐园。

玩了一天,回到家以后,皮特一直沉浸在云霄飞车和旋转木马的回忆中,一直到凌晨三点才睡。嘴里不停地念叨着"六旗世界,六旗世界"。

"确实很奇怪,"特尔斯夫人回忆道,"我们一夜都没睡,一直看着沃克。真的很有意思。我心里很高兴。" 特尔斯夫人一边说着一边笑了起来。

*Navigating Transitions*
风雨同舟

2006 年

那一年，皮特所在的教会进行了扩建，主楼旁边加了一个用于"特尔斯主日"活动的附属建筑。当大家匆匆去参加活动的时候，皮特却在主楼的石门外徘徊。

"到这边来，到这边来，"特尔斯夫人向皮特边招手边喊道，"我们的活动已经搬到了这里，我们不再去那个老地方了。"可是皮特就是不动。他看着那扇大门，脸上毫无表情。

"他不说话，但是很清楚，他感到困惑，他还是想去教会的那个老地方参加活动，像皮特这样的人是很难适应新环境的，"特尔斯夫人喝了一口茶，看着沃克说，"有时，他们需要多一点儿时间。"

特尔斯夫人接着解释了皮特是怎样不愿意交朋友，并且总是想念在上大学的妹妹。特尔斯夫人问她的儿子："你想夏丽吗？"皮特点了点头。

2007 年

特尔斯夫人讲着自闭症的故事，皮特看着桌子上的薯条，轻微挤着他妈妈。皮特不怎么讲话，只是沉浸在餐厅播放的音乐之中。

"皮特 13 岁的时候，我第一次带他去了纽约。那天，没有人照顾他，所以我就带上他，他妹妹，和他的朋友一起去了纽约。"

皮 特

特尔斯夫人回忆道。

"我女儿特别喜欢音乐剧。所以我们看了好几个百老汇节目，包括'西部故事''狮子王''爱情之旅'，当然还有'玛玛米亚'。皮特特别喜欢'玛玛米亚'。"

这时皮特挠了挠头皮，好像想起了这个他最喜欢的节目。

特尔斯夫人说皮特和别的自闭症患者不一样。皮特有很强的容忍噪音的能力。在观看百老汇节目中，皮特像正常人一样，被允许坐在普通观众席，服务人员在门口欢迎他，给了他节目单，并且引领他到座位上。

但对皮特讲，纽约之行的最亮点不是看节目，而是坐公交车和地铁。在公交车上，皮特激动地看着一座座摩天大楼和一条条繁忙的街道。在地铁站，他刷了公交卡，挤过了转动门通道。我们坐了一个小时地铁才从中城来到中国城，一路上一直看着外面的精彩世界。

"他喜欢地铁，因为对他来讲，坐地铁有点像到了六旗世界的感觉。"特尔斯夫人看着皮特轻轻地笑了起来。

"让我们感到惊讶的是，纽约人不是像我们想象的那样粗暴尖刻。我们在纽约的时候，每个人都愿意把座位让给皮特，甚至包括那些穿着宽大毛衣戴着耳机的人。"

纽约人很友善，特别是在时报广场的人们。在那里，我们排队买票。售票处的工作人员看到皮特挤在长队中很不方便，

就直接带我们到队的最前面,于是我们最先买到了票。

"在节目中,尽管皮特可以行走和活动,工作人员还是提供了残疾人座位给我们。他们是这么有爱心。真是太感谢他们了。"

2008 年至 2014 年

"自闭症患者常常在模仿方面有困难。在爱顿特殊学校,老师们教皮特做模仿动作,像拍手等。然而掌握这些模仿动作,对皮特讲也是困难的。老师们给我们介绍了一个叫'应用行为分析'(ABA)的教学方法。就是通过正面强化来学习的方法。每当皮特在学校或者在家里成功地进行了模仿,我们就奖励他。从传统方法转到 ABA 方法,不仅帮助皮特更有效地学习,而且也改善了皮特的行为和心智。我觉得每一个自闭症患者的家长都应该试试这个方法。"

在这期间,特尔斯夫人还注意到皮特开始不在意别人对他的看法。当别人注视他或对他指指点点的时候,皮特也不在意。

"重要的是,有一个时间点,他开始不在意别人怎么想,怎么想是他们的问题。"

2015 年

去年,皮特从爱顿自闭症服务中心的继续关怀课程毕业了。作为一个 22 岁的年轻人,皮特没有受过正规的教育,但他却做

皮特

起了一些简单的工作：包装宠物动物的食品，准备邮件和清扫房间。尽管他在学业上有困难，通过上班，皮特还是能够掌握一些基本的操作技术，比如用吸尘器和做饭。有一段时间，他还给大都会剧院折叠节目单。

皮特有了一些基本的技能，但他的自闭症还是很严重的。他需要老师和治疗人员的指导帮助。所以特尔斯夫人给皮特申请了住宿项目，在那里皮特可以得到终身的他所需要的照顾。

"申请住宿项目的过程是漫长的，因为位子有限和申请的人太多，我们得知皮特要等到30岁的时候才能得到一个位子。当然，我想让皮特马上就能住进去，但是住宿项目是根据每个人的需要和病的严重程度决定先后顺序。我的儿子能帮忙也很听话，在家照顾他还不是特别困难。"特尔斯夫人说，"但是对其他自闭症患者的家长，照顾他们的孩子可能就特别困难。"

特尔斯夫人叹了口气，在不安中说了起来，"我们真的希望皮特有一个永久的家。尽管这听起来有点不正常，我这么说吧，如果我和我丈夫明天死于车祸，我们想确认会有人照顾皮特，我不想让皮特18岁的妹妹照顾他，因为她要有自己的生活。不管怎样，新泽西还是很领先的，我不希望每件事做起来都太官僚作风。比如我们有问题，我们希望政府的服务更加简捷方便。

皮特突然点起了头，好像很同情他的妈妈。

特尔斯夫人慈爱地看着皮特说："有时，我觉得皮特并不

关心我,我感觉他不会回报我对他的爱,可能他不理解这些。你知道吗,我这样照顾皮特已经25年了,我有点儿累了。有一天,我正喝着从当肯麦圈店买来的咖啡,皮特要我把咖啡倒掉,他要玩那个盛咖啡的杯子。他有时不考虑我的感觉,做一些莽撞的事情。"特尔斯夫人拿了一张餐巾纸,擦去了皮特领口的调料酱,以免弄脏海军蓝衬衣。

特尔斯夫人最后说道:"说到底,皮特和我,只想做我们自己,有一天,我问皮特,他想不想像他妹妹一样去上大学,他回答说:'不,我只想和你在一起。'"

"尽管他自己知道他和别人不一样,但是他不在意。他喜欢他的生活方式。他不想像他妹妹一样,和朋友在一起,或者去上大学,不和我们生活在一起。别人会议论我们,他们总是这样。说实话,何必在意哪? 再说一遍,这是他们的问题,不是我们的问题。我觉得我们生活得很好很幸福。"

Further Reading 附录

# Introduction: Autism and Families

James Ball, Ed.D., BCBA-D
Immediate Past Chair, National Board of Directors, Autism Society
Interagency Autism Coordinating Committee - Community Member

When Michelle first came to me and said she wanted to write a book, I thought, "what could she write about that would be relevant and have an impact?" She could write about behavior, social skills, but what would really make a difference? Then it came to me, "how about parent stories of their individual journey with autism?" Michelle had access to many different families based on her summer internship. She could write their stories. Autism has so many different faces and this would be a good way to document some of them. This is very similar to my book, Early Intervention and Autism: Real-Life Questions, Real-Life Answers, helping Parents navigate a very confusing system. These stories can help families understand autism from a very personal place.

Navigating Transitions
风雨同舟

Michelle then asked me to do her introduction and I decided that what I wanted to add to her book is some suggestions for families starting their journey with autism. I wrote an article for the Autism/Aspergers Digest magazine that did just that, I would like to share that with you:

Autism: A Whole Family Condition

A great many people are now looking at autism from a "whole body" perspective, not just from a behavioral or biomedical point of view. Cathy Pratt, Director of the nationally renowned and respected Indiana Resource Center for Autism, has also referred to it as a "whole family" condition. Autism's impact on the family, on moms, dads, siblings, grandparents, aunts, and uncles, is tangible and can be devastating. Those of us who provide programs and services – including education - need to be diligent in helping the family, as well as the child, find ways to be healthy and work together to ensure success for everyone. The happier the family, the happier the child will become. However, as most of us realize, this is easier said than done. And that is precisely why we must make a concerted effort to address family needs while we are helping the child.

Moms and dads are heartfelt in their desire to help their child, but they approach the situation from very different angles, ones that are often at odds with each other. Many parents neither recognize nor accept how these different gender roles and perceptions can affect the way each person relates to the diagnosis itself, to understanding autism and making decisions about treatment. Often the result is both parents feel alienated from one another and the child's education becomes delegated to Mom, who willingly or not, becomes responsible for learning about autism, unearthing possible sources of assistance, and deciding on treatment. Dad, on theotherhand, assumestheresponsibilityforfinancingthem, often staying an arm's length away from becoming more in volved in care and treatment.

Couplescaneasilydriftapartatthisdelicatejuncture. Dad goes off to work each morning and Mom starts to resent his "freedom." He doesn't have to deal with the child's relentless meltdowns. He doesn't have to clean up yet another mess the child created, or deal with strangers' stares or whispers when the grocery store is out of the child's favorite cereal. For her, autism requires her attention 24/7 and becomes a never ending (and often thankless) job. She often feels alone and unappreciated. In turn, Dad starts feeling alienated himself. Without regular, direct exposure to the child, he doesn't learn how to handle autism. He feels inadequate when he tries. He resents that his wife devotes all her time to the

child and no longer has time for him. As Mom reaches out to others for information and support more and more, he no longer feels needed except for his paycheck. Moms can inadvertently shut dads out of the information loop, setting up a pattern of learned helplessness - the inability to do something based on lack of exposure or experience at doing it. Every year for the past ten years, I have had the great for tune of being involved with a presentation at the Autism So ciety of America's Annual Conference, called "For Father's Only." Even though this presentation is restricted to men and focuses on the thoughts, and yes feelings of fathers, this past year we invited back a mom to speak at our presentation. She was an "action mom" who had tried some of the ideas we discussed last year and found them to be a lifesaver for her marriage. The top five strategies are listed below. These are things not only for dad to do, but that involve the whole family. They strengthen the family unit and in so doing, create an environment in which the child with autism can thrive and grow.

5 Ways to Keep a Family Healthy

1. Go out as a family once a week. Pick places that are fun for everyone. In the beginning try to go out during "down times," when fewer people are around (especially a good idea if your child has sensory issues). Try activities such

as roller-skating or bowling, fishing, swimming, going on a hike and/or a picnic. Do the same activity over and over, so your spectrum child gets familiar with the routine and the environment. Let the child experience success in family outings before venturing into other activities that mightrequire greater patience or skill sets.

2. Prioritize the needs of the family and schedule times to tackle them. As the parent, you do have to be "on" all the time. Pick out those things that most directly affect the family and handle them in order of their importance. For example, if your child on the spectrum is having issues during meal times, schedule a time when you can teach him needed social or behavior skills during meal time. Your older, typical child is having trouble with homework? Schedule a time when you can give that child your complete attention and help. This also goes for your spouse; be sure you both attend to eachother' sneedsfortimealone, caring, andaffection. Schedule a time for that too.

3. Start a Family Game Night. This is not only a great way to teach the child with ASD important social skills, it gives everyone an opportunity to "hang out" together. It's also a great way to get siblings involved with their brother or sister with autism.

4. Eat meals together. Perhaps it's not every night, but as

often as you can, try to eat meals together. This familygathering can be a time to learn about each other's day and share information about what's happening within the family. And it's another opportunity for the child to practice daily living/social skills!

5. Parents: Give yourself a break on a regular basis. Go out together as a couple and/or alone. Do something fun or relaxing. Feed your spirit and your personality. It could be as simple as taking an hour to go to the local book store and read a book (even on autism if you like), or take a class in yoga or painting. Or it could be as complex as attending a national conference on autism every year, or taking a vacation with your friends. Consider yourself and your own needs as im portant as are those of the child with ASD. You need to find ways to refresh yourself and not feel "consumed" by autism or the situation you find yourself in at the time.

If you view autism as a dis-ability, it will dis-able your family and your lives. See it rather as a different ability, recognizing that it affects the entire family (even the dog). Learn to notice the positive aspects of autism. They are there; you just need to see them. When things get out of control and you lose your direction, seek outside help. Support groups, a good friend, trained counselors or a spiritual connection are all ways to navigate the often choppy seas of life in general, but can be life preservers for families of children with ASD. Find ways that help you stay afloat – as an individual, as a couple and as a family – when dark skies loom overhead. Always keep your focus on the child and his needs, but not by neglecting yourself or other members of your family. You are all equally important. To truly help your child, you often need to first find ways to help yourself accept and love him, autism included. Your family is only as strong as its weakest link.

Autism is a marathon, not a short race and then it's over. It is essential that parents do whatever they need to do to stay fit, conserve energy and pace themselves so they can be positive, connected and effective over the long haul. Your child is counting on you to keep him in the race and teach him to run to the best of his ability. This will only happen if the family is healthy. If you believe you can do it, you will. If you believe your child can do it, he will. If you believe your family can it, you all will. Just believe.

I hope this helps!! Now, explore what each of these families have experienced and understand that every person's experience is different.

# Increasing autism prevalence in metropolitan New Jersey

Walter Zahorodny , Josephine Shenouda, Sandra Howell,
Nancy Scotto Rosato , Bo Peng and Uday Mehta

## Abstract

High baseline autism spectrum disorder prevalence estimates in New Jersey led to a follow-up surveillance. The objectives were to determine autism spectrum disorder prevalence in the year 2006 in New Jersey and to identify changes in the prevalence of autism spectrum disorder or in the characteristics of the children with autism spectrum disorder, between 2002 and 2006. The cohorts included 30,570 children, born in 1998 and 28,936 children, born in 1994, residing in Hudson, Union, and Ocean counties, New Jersey. Point prevalence estimates by sex, ethnicity, autism spectrum disorder subtype, and previous autism spectrum disorder diagnosis were determined. For 2006, a total of 533 children with autism spectrum disorder were identified, consistent with

prevalence of 17.4 per 1000 (95% confidence interval = 15.9–18.9), indicating a significant increase in the autism spectrum disorder prevalence ($p < 0.001$), between 2002 (10.6 per 1000) and 2006. The rise in autism spectrum disorder was broad, affecting major demographic groups and subtypes. Boys with autism spectrum disorder outnumbered girls by nearly 5:1. Autism spectrum disorder prevalence was higher among White children than children of other ethnicities. Additional studies are needed to specify the influence of better awareness of autism spectrum disorder prevalence estimates and to identify possible autism spectrum disorder risk factors. More resources are necessary to address the needs of individuals affected by autism spectrum disorder.

**Keywords**

autism, autism spectrum disorder prevalence, developmental disabilities surveillance, epidemiology, New Jersey, population-based, public health monitoring

**Introduction**

Autism spectrum disorder (ASD) is a complex developmental disorder characterized by impairment in social and communication ability and restricted, anomalous, or repeti

tive behavior. ASD is evident before 3 years of age ( Yeargin-Allsopp et al., 2003 ) ; variable in expression ( Lord et al., 2006; Prior et al., 1998 ) ; more common in males ( Newschaffer et al., 2007; Wing and Potter, 2002 ) ; and frequently accompanied by deficits in attention, cognition, and sensory-processing ( Gillberg and Billstedt, 2000 ) . Although there is a heritable dimension to ASD ( Bailey et al., 1995; Folstein and Rutter, 1977; Lichtenstein et al., 2010; Weiss, 2009 ) , neither genetic nor environmental factors have been successfully elucidated ( Gilman et al., 2011; Hallmayer et al., 2011; Levy et al., 2011; Liu et al., 2010 ) . The functional limitations of individuals with ASD and the life-long need for health, education, and support services ( Honberg et al., 2009 ) underscore the public health signifi cance of this disorder.

Not long ago, ASD was thought to affect one in 2000 children ( Fombonne, 2009 ) . Since 1990, the number of persons receiving services for autism has increased substantially ( California Department of Developmental Services, 1999, 2003; Newschaffer et al., 2005 ) , as have ASD estimates defined by epidemiologic studies ( Baird et al., 2006; Chakrabarti and Fombonne, 2001; Hertz-Picciotto andDelwiche, 2009; Honda et al., 2005 ) . However, significant controversy continues regarding whether the observed increases reflect true change in ASD risk, expansion of the definition, increased awareness, or other factors (Blaxill, 2004; Charman, 2002; Fombonne, 2009; Gernsbacher et al., 2005). Repeated, population-based surveillance in specific geographic areas, using birth year as a reference, may provide the best basis for inferring ASD prevalence and trends. Using such an approach, baseline ASD estimates from two cycles of monitoring by the Centers for Disease Control and Prevention (CDC) — Autism and Developmental Disabilities Monitoring (ADDM) Network, among 8-year-old children, born in 1992 and 1994 and residing in multiple US regions, averaged 6.7 per 1000 (range = 4.5–9.9) and 6.6 per 1000 (range = 3.3–10.6) in 2000 and 2002, respectively (CDC, 2007a, 2007b). However, ASD prevalence in New Jersey (9.9 and 10.6 per 1000), determined by the same method, was significantly higher ($p < 0.001$) than in all other ADDM states, in both years (CDC, 2007a, 2007b). For 2006, the ADDM Network (not including New Jersey) identified a marked increase in ASD prevalence to 9.0 per 1000 (range = 4.2–12.1), over the preceding 4 years (CDC, 2009). In light of the high rates of ASD identified in New Jersey for 2000 and 2002 and the increases in ASD prevalence identified by the ADDM Network for 2006, the goals of this study were to provide updated estimates of ASD prevalence in the New Jersey Metropolitan

Area (NJMA), using identical methods and procedures, for comparison of ASD prevalence, between 2002 and 2006.

## Methods

Study region and population

ASD surveillance was conducted in Hudson, Essex, Union, and Ocean counties, New Jersey, a densely populated, urban-suburban, area of 2.4 million, within the largest US metropolis. The region includes three of the state's largest cities and over 75 communities, encompassing an ethnically diverse population (43% White, 25% Black, 26% Hispanic, and 6% others; United States. Bureau of the Census, 1991) and representing the widest range of socioeconomic strata. Surveillance was restricted to (8-year-old) children born in 1998, residing in the study region, in 2006. The study was approved by the New Jersey Medical School (NJMS) Institutional Review Board (IRB) and implemented with the cooperation of local school districts, developmental and behavioral health centers, as well as state education and health authorities. The cases were linked to New Jersey birth certificate data, to confirm additional demographic information.

Children with ASD were identified using the two phase ADDM method of ASD ascertainment through (a) active, multiple-source screening and (2) independent case

Further Reading 附录

determination. The surveillance method has been described extensively elsewhere (CDC, 2007a, 2007b, 2009).

Case definitions

Autistic disorder (AD) was defined as a pattern of behaviors, as described in evaluation records by qualified professionals, consistent with the Diagnostic and Statistical Manual of Mental Disorders (4th ed., text rev.; DSM-IV-TR) diagnostic criteria for AD, at any time, through age 8 years. Specifically, AD was defined as a case in which a child shows six or more features of autism, including two or more signs of social impairment and one or more signs each of communication and behavioral impairment, as well as documented developmental concern before the age of 3 years. ASD-not otherwise specified (ASD-NOS) was defined as a case in which the child met the DSM-IV-TR criteria for pervasive developmental disorders–not otherwise specified (PDD-NOS) or Asperger's disorder and also satisfied the study-specific requirement that at least one documented behavior be of such quality or intensity to be highly indicative of ASD. An evaluation record was an assessment conducted by a professional for determination of the need for special education services or to diagnose a developmental, behavioral, or neurological disorder. A qualified professional was defined as a medical, psychological, or other professional

with specialized training in the observation of children with developmental disorders. Regression was documented by statements in professional evaluations indicating that the child lost previously acquired language or social skills. Children with an intelligence quotient (IQ) greater than 85, on a standard intelligence test, were defined to have average or above average cognitive ability. Children with an IQ between 71 and 85 were considered to have borderline cognitive impairment (BCI). Children with an IQ of 70 or below were classified as having cognitive impairment (CI).

Phase 1—case ascertainment

Records of children educated under any special education classification and/or receiving clinical evaluation or treatment under one or more of 80 International Classification of Diseases, 9th Revision (ICD-9) disorder codes were reviewed. Records of children with documented or sus pected ASD diagnoses or with one or more description (s) of social impairment associated with autism were abstracted. The abstracted information included demographic and developmental data, clinical findings, including diagnoses, educational classification and placement information, verbatim descriptions of behavior and development, psychometric findings, service, and treatment data. The information from health and education sources was linked and organized as a

Further Reading 附录

composite, nonidentifiable, chronological case file per child.

Figure 1. Study diagram. (a) Describes the 2006 study population, ASD was found to be 17.4 per 1000 children and (b) describes the curtailed population in 2006, which is used in comparison to data from SY2002, ASD prevalence was found to be slightly higher than 17.6 per 1000 children.

ASD: autism spectrum disorder; SY: study year

Phase 2—clinician review and analysis

Subjects' case information was scored and analyzed by certified child development specialists (one developmental pediatrician, two psychologists, and one learning disabilities consultant), each with more than 10 years of professional experience and more than 5 years of expertise using the CDC-ADDM DSM-IV-TR–based Clinician Review coding procedures to determine ASD case status (Case, Suspected, Does Not Qualify (DNQ)) and ASD Type (AD, ASD-NOS). Children were identified as having documented ASD if they received a diagnosis of any ASD froma qualified professional. Prior to the analytic phase, expert reviewers established interrater reliability according to the CDC-ADDM standard of >95% agreement for ASD case definition and >80% agreement for other scored features. Ongoing interrater reliability testing was conducted on a random, blinded 10% sample of reviewed records. The percent agreement for final case definition was very good (range: 91%–100% (kappa range: 0.8–1.0)).

Analytic methods

The total population of 8-year-olds in the surveillance region was 31,069. Seventy-five of 78 school districts participated with the study, representing 30,570 children (98.2%) in the region, according to the National Center for Health Statistics (NCHS) vintage 2007 postcensal data. The prevalence estimates were calculated using the total number of 8-year-olds who resided in the 75 participating districts. NCHS datasets provided population counts by county, year of birth, sex, and ethnicity. Ethnicity-specific estimates were calculated for the categories: White non Hispanic; Black non-Hispanic; Hispanic; and Others, which encompassed children of Asian and/or American

Indian ancestry. Poisson's distribution was used to calculate 95% confidence intervals (CIs) for prevalence rates. For the purposes of comparing ASD prevalence between 2002 and 2006, an adjusted set representing only data from districts participating both years was established and analyzed (Figure 1). Chi-square tests were used to compare prevalence estimates and rate ratios, and percentage changes were used to compare changes between 2002 and 2006. A maximum value of $p < 0.05$ determined statistical significance. Because ASD prevalence is determined on the basis of information contained in evaluation records, multiple factors that could influence the estimate, including variability in access, the effects of migration, and missing or incomplete records, were assessed.

Results

Overall ASD prevalence study year 2006

In a population of 30,570 eight-year-olds, the clinical and educational records of 3332 children from 75 school districts were reviewed. Subsequently, records of 923 children (3% of the total 8-year-old population) met the conditions for abstraction and were analyzed, leading to the identification of 533 children with study-determined ASD, a prevalence of 17.4 per 1000 (Table 1). Two children with Rett's syndrome were identified but not included in the prevalence count. ASD prevalence was much higher among boys (28.3 per 1000) than girls (5.8 per 1000) and highest among White non-Hispanic boys, ranging from 30.4 to 39.1 per 1000. A total of 413 (77%) children satisfied the full diagnostic criteria for AD, and 367 (69%) had a documented (previous) ASD diagnosis from a community provider. Agreement between previous ASD diagnosis and ASD case status by the surveillance method was 99%. Five hundred nine ASD children (95%) received special education service in 2006, and 224

(44%) were educated under an autism classification.

Comparison between New Jersey areas surveyed in 2002 and 2006

To reduce the possibility of changes in population affecting our prevalence estimates, we compared ASD prevalence across the 58 New Jersey communities that participated in both surveillance years. Between 2002 and 2006, ASD prevalence increased from 10.8 to 17.6 per 1000 ($p < 0.001$; Table 1; Figure 2). Higher ASD rates were evident across most demographic and functional categories. ASD prevalence among boys rose from 17.0 to 28.7 per 1000 ($p < 0.001$) and increased from 4.1 to 5.9 per 1000 among girls ($p < 0.05$). The ASD prevalence rates between girls and boys were significantly different in 2002 and 2006 ($p < 0.001$). However, though the 2002–2006 rate ratio change of 1.71 for boys was greater than the rate ratio change observed for girls (1.41), the overlapping 95% CIs between boys and girls indicate that the difference is not statistically significant (Table 1). Likewise, the ASD rates rose significantly among Black non-Hispanic, White non-Hispanic, and Hispanic children (90%, 66%, and 51%, respectively; Table 1; Figure 2). While the number of children satisfying the criteria for AD increased, the proportion of ASD children with regression was unchanged (Table 2). Rising ASD prevalence was also

reflected in greater numbers of children diagnosed with ASD by a community professional (6.7–11.7 per 1000 (p < 0.001)) and children educated under an autism eligibility (4.5–7.4 per 1000 (p < 0.001); Table 1; Figure 3).

To assess possible influences on ASD prevalence, multiple factors representing case characteristics and data completeness were compared (Table 2). In-migration was stable during the period. Measures reflecting data quality, including the percentage of ASD children receiving special education services (98%–95%) and the proportion of children with evaluations from both clinical and educational sources (83%–86%), were uniformly high (Table 2), while the number of unavailable cases or cases with incomplete information was small across years (unpublished findings). The abstraction proportion, representing the percent of the total population whose records underwent review and analysis, increased significantly during the period, but a smaller proportion of analyzed cases satisfied the ASD case definition. The ages of earliest professional evaluation and earliest documented ASD diagnosis declined between 2002 and 2006 (Table 2).

Discussion

Just as recent epidemiologic studies have converged at a 1% estimated level of ASD prevalence (Baird et al., 2006;

CDC, 2009; Fombonne, 2009; Honda et al., 2005), this study suggests that ASD prevalence may be closer to 2%, in some US regions. Using a comprehensive, population-based method, we determined that 1 in 57 eight-year-olds in the NJMA, in 2006, had an ASD. While this estimate is higher than the rates from other US areas using the same case-finding method (CDC, 2009), higher than the rates derived from nationally representative health survey data for the same period (Kogan et al., 2009), and higher than baseline ASD prevalence in the same region 4 years earlier (CDC, 2009), the overall ASD prevalence of 17.4 per 1000 is in the range of recent ASD estimates from Cambridgeshire, United Kingdom (Baron-Cohen et al., 2009), and Goyang, South Korea (Kim et al., 2011). Higher ASD prevalence in New Jersey in comparison to other US regions, across surveillance cycles, may be a function of more detailed information in New Jersey records, leading to more complete ASD ascertainment. However, additional effects from as-yet-unknown demographic and/or environmental factors cannot be ruled out. Consistent with multiple studies (CDC, 2009; Parner et al., 2008; Posserud et al., 2006), nearly five times as many

boys than girls were affected, representing an absolute level of male ASD prevalence (1 in 35) that is startling, if not unprecedented (Kim et al., 2011), and underscoring the need for further research into the sex-based differences in autism. In our population, ASD prevalence also varied by ethnicity, with White non-Hispanic children showing the highest levels of ASD, consistent with some epidemiologic studies (CDC, 2007a, 2007b; Kogan et al., 2009) and contrary to others (Fombonne, 2001; Hillman et al., 2000; Yeargin-Allsopp et al., 2003). The observed differences in ethnic distribution of ASD may reflect variations in genetic susceptibility, environmental risk, ascertainment, or combinations of these factors. Regardless, further consideration of demographic influences on ASD prevalence is indicated, especially to understand disparities in ASD identification and diagnosis (Durkin et al., 2010; Levy et al., 2011; Mandell et al., 2009; Thomas et al., 2011). Following on stable baseline ASD estimates for 2000 and 2002, the upward shift in ASD prevalence in 2006 was unexpected. However, the increase was substantial and affected children across demographic groups, similar in magnitude (63%) to the increases in autism special education classification (65%) and community-diagnosed ASD in our region (75%), and consistent with the average increase in ASD prevalence (57%), reported by the US ADDM Network sites, between 2002 and 2006. In the absence of a significant change in definition, policy, or service availability relevant to ASD, it is difficult to understand why

all indicators of autism prevalence would have escalated 50%–75% during the period.

A number of factors may have influenced our estimates. For example, enhanced awareness and improved diagnosis of ASD could have contributed to the observed changes. Comparing the 2002 and 2006 ASD case characteristics, we observed a reduction in the median age of ASD diagnosis and an increased number of children with previously diagnosed ASD, two gauges of （community） awareness that might have influenced the determination of ASD prevalence. However, the shift in age of earliest ASD diagnosis was relatively modest （4.5 months）, while the proportion of previously diagnosed ASD children was unchanged over the period, indicating that these specific factors may not have exerted a substantial influence on our prevalence estimation. Alternatively, improving awareness of ASD might have been expressed through enhanced recognition of ASD in children from minority groups or among children with higher cognitive functioning. While we did identify increased numbers of Black and Hispanic children with ASD, as well as more ASD children with borderline IQ and average or above average IQ, in 2006, significant increases in diagnosed and study-defined ASD were also evident among White children and children with CI, suggesting a broadly based escalation of ASD, rather than an increase reflecting improved case-finding in specific populations. Another possibility is that the ascertainment method was overinclusive and/or prone to inflation over time due to increasing identification of borderline or atypical ASD cases. Regarding the first point, a recent validation study (Avchen et al., 2011) found that the (CDC-ADDM) ascertainment method is conservative, with high specificity and low sensitivity and, therefore, more likely to underestimate ASD prevalence than to overstate it. Furthermore, contrary to expectation, comparing 2002 and 2006 estimates, we found significant increase in the proportion of children satisfying the criteria for AD but not in children identified with ASD-NOS. Interestingly, 70%–75% of 8-year-old ASD children, across all surveillance cycles, satisfied the strict diagnostic criteria for AD, in keeping with the sub type distribution described by some studies (Bertrand et al., 2001; CDC, 2007a, 2007b, 2009) and at variance with others (Chakrabarti and Fombonne, 2001; Fombonne, 2003). Since the ADDM surveillance method analyzes detailed,

subject-specific, information across multiple evaluations, it is very likely to have a more robust array of information and to confirm AD more frequently than studies that define ASD subtype by one or two evaluative contacts.

To ensure the comparability of ASD estimates over time, we maintained CDC-ADDM ascertainment methods,

case definitions, and analytic procedures, including quality assurance operations, across the surveillance cycles. The total population of 8-year-olds decreased in three of four surveillance counties between 2002 and 2006, but our access to multiple high-quality health and education records was consistently high, resulting in maximum levels of exposure to potential cases. Though the study was not designed to evaluate the effects of migration patterns on ASD, the base population of the NJMA is stable and the in-migration level is low. In 2002 and 2006, 84% and 82% of ASD cases, respectively, matched to New Jersey birth certificates, suggesting that in-migration did not have a significant influence on the overall prevalence estimate or on changing prevalence, over time. To reduce the possibility of error in calculating change in prevalence, we only compared districts that participated with ASD surveillance, both years. Our analyses of data quality showed high levels of completeness and no significant difference on most indicators, between the two cycles (unpublished findings). While the number of records reviewed on behalf of ASD surveillance did not vary significantly over cycles, the number of abstracted cases increased from 419 in 2002 to 807 in 2006, representing a significant increase in the proportion (1.4%–3.1%) that underwent expert analysis. It is difficult to determine the extent to which the change in abstraction proportion affected the 2006 prevalence estimate. In previous cycles of ASD surveillance by the ADDM Network, the abstraction proportion ranged between 1% and 3% without systematic effect on ASD prevalence (CDC, 2007a, 2007b). On the other hand, it stands to reason that high levels of ASD awareness and higher levels of ASD diagnosis will serve to an enlarged scope of ascertainment and may affect the prevalence estimate.

Overall, this study shows a high and increasing number of children in the NJMA affected by ASD. Some of the increase may be a function of improved awareness and diagnosis. However, the possibility of an increase in ASD prevalence, due to changing risk, cannot be ruled out. Ongoing ASD surveillance using the same epidemiologic method by the entire ADDM Network and New Jersey is essential to monitor possible, future, changes in the expression or prevalence of autism and to allow the comparisons that will clarify ASD risk and ascertainment factors. Even in regions like New Jersey, where the population has good to excellent access to clinical specialists and where children are served by a universal, well-funded, public education system, a significant minority of children with ASD are not diagnosed (with ASD) before age 8. This gap in identification has been consistent across time and US surveillance sites and points to the fact that administrative or registrybased estimates of ASD prevalence that are based only on already-diagnosed children will underestimate the actual number of individuals with ASD.

This study has a number of strengths, deriving from the design and the large, diverse, nature of the population. Consistent implementation of an active, multiplesource ascertainment strategy, in a well-specified region, provides the most accurate ASD prevalence estimates and the best opportunity to evaluate changes in prevalence. The detailed case-specific information derived from multiple sources allows for identification of ASD in children without a previous diagnosis, thereby ensuring the most complete ASD estimates. Linkage of highly detailed case-specific data with birth certificate, census files, and other sets permits additional analyses that may lead to the identification of ASD risk factors and to appreciation of disparities in service to ASD children.

Some limitations of the study should be pointed out. Only children identified for special education or for clinical (developmental) services came under the purview of our surveillance. Some children with Asperger's syndrome or high-functioning ASD are educated in general education settings and did not come to the attention of their school district or our study, thereby leading to underestimate ASD prevalence. Also, since the surveillance method is able to analyze a large amount of detailed information across multiple professionals contained in evaluation records, while an approach based on direct clinical assessment is limited to defining ASD type from observations by one professional at a single point in time, our method may overestimate the prevalence of AD, relative to atypical ASD.

Regardless of whether one acknowledges an increased ASD prevalence, all the epidemiologic and administrative studies confirm that ASD is now among the most common, severe, developmental disorders. It is too soon to know at what point ASD prevalence will plateau. As more children with

ASD are identified, more resources will be required to assist the affected individuals and their families. Additional research is needed to assess the factors bearing on increasing ASD prevalence and to identify the etiological factors of this key disorder. The multiple-source, active, case-finding method can be especially effective for monitoring behaviorally defined disorders like ASD and may be fruitfully extended to other developmental, learning, and/or psychiatric disorders.

## Acknowledgements

W. Zahorodny is responsible for the integrity of the data. All authors approved the manuscript's contents. The comments and assistance of Jon Baio EdS and Catherine Rice PhD of the CDC-National Center for Birth Defects and

Developmental Disabilities is gratefully acknowledged. The analytic and technical expertise of Audrey Mars MD, Mildred Waale LDTC, Arline Fusco PsyD, Katherine Hempstead PhD, Paul Zumoff PhD and Rita Baltus MD, as well as the cooperative support and participation of the New Jersey Departments of Health and Education and the many school districts and health centers in our region is gratefully acknowledged.

Declaration of conflicting interest

The authors report no conflicts of interest. The findings and conclusions in this report are those of the authors and do not necessarily represent the position of the New Jersey Governor's Council for Biomedical Research and Treatment of Autism or the CDC.

Funding

This study was supported by a grant from the New Jersey Governor's Council for Biomedical Research and Treatment of Autism and by technical support from the CDC to the senior author.

## References

American Community Survey (2009) New Jersey U.S Census. Available at: http://wonder.cdc.gov/bridged-race-population.html

Avchen RN, Wiggins LD, Devine O, et al. (2011) Evaluation of a records-review surveillance system used to determine the prevalence of autism spectrum disorders. Journal of Autism and Developmental Disorders 41 (2): 227–236.

Bailey A, Le Couteur A, Gottesman I, et al. (1995) Autism as a strong genetic disorders: evidence from a British twin study. Psychological Medicine 25: 63–77.

Baird G, Simonoff E, Pickles A, et al. (2006) Prevalence of disorders of the autism spectrum in a population cohort of children in South Thames: the special needs and autism project (SNAP). Lancet 368: 210–215.

Baron-Cohen S, Scott FJ, Allison C, et al. (2009) Prevalence of autism-spectrum conditions: UK school-based population study. British Journal of Psychiatry 194 (6): 500–509. Erratum in British Journal of Psychiatry 195(2): 182.

Blaxill MF (2004) What's going on? The question of time trends in autism. Public Health Reports 119: 536–551.

California Department of Developmental Services (1999) Changes in the population of persons with autism and pervasive development disorders in California Department of Developmental disorders in California's Developmental Services System: 1987 through 1998. A report to the legislature. Sacramento, CA: CA Department of Developmental Services. The 1999 Report, Changes in the Population of Persons with Autism and Pervasive Developmental Disorders in California's Developmental Services System can be downloaded at http://www.dds. ca.gov/autism/pdf/autismreport_1999.pdf.

California Department of Developmental Services (2003) Autistic spectrum disorders: changes in the California caseload. An update: 1999 through 2002. Sacramento, CA: CA Department of Developmental Services.

Centers of Disease Control and Prevention (2007a) Prevalence of autism spectrum disorders—autism and developmental disabilities monitoring network, six sites, United States, 2000. Morbidity & Mortality Weekly Report 56 (1): 1–11.

Centers of Disease Control and Prevention (2007b) Prevalence of autism spectrum disorders—autism and developmental disabilities monitoring network, 14 sites, United States, 2002 (In: Surveillance Summaries, 9 February 2007). Morbidity & Mortality Weekly Report 56 (1): 12–28.

Centers of Disease Control and Prevention (2009) Prevalence of autism spectrum disorders—autism and developmental disabilities monitoring network, 14 sites, United States, 2006. Morbidity & Mortality Weekly Report 58 (10): 1–20.

Chakrabarti S and Fombonne E (2001) Pervasive developmental disorders in preschool children. Journal of the American Medical Association 285: 3093–3099.

Charman T (2002) The prevalence of autism spectrum disorders: recent evidence and future challenges. European Child & Adolescent Psychiatry 11: 249–256.

Durkin MS, Maenner MJ and Meaney FJ (2010) Socioeconomic inequality in the prevalence of autism spectrum disorder evidence from a U.S. cross-sectional study. PLoS One 5 (7): e11551.

Folstein S and Rutter M (1977) Infantile autism: a gender study of 21 twin pairs. Journal of Child Psychology and Psychiatry 18 (4): 297–321.

Fombonne E (2001) Epidemiological investigations of autism and other pervasive developmental disorders. In: Lord C (ed.) Educating Children with Autism. Washington, DC: National Academy of Sciences Press, pp. 21–31.

Fombonne E (2003) The prevalence of autism. Journal of

the American Medical Association 289（1）: 87-89.

Fombonne E（2009） Epidemiology of pervasive developmental disorders. Pediatric Research 65（6）: 591-598.

Gernsbacher MA, Dawson M and Goldsmith HH （2005） Three reasons not to believe in an autism epidemic. Current Directions in Psychological Science 14: 55-58.

Gillberg C and Billstedt E （2000） Autism and Asperger syndrome: coexistence with other clinical disorders. Acta Psychiatrica Scandinavica 102: 321-330.

Gilman S, Iossifov I, Levy D, et al.（2011） Rare de novo variants associated with autism implicate a large functional network of genes involved in formation and function of synapses. Neuron 70（5）: 898-907.

Hallmayer J, Cleveland S, Torres A, et al.（2011） Genetic heritability and shared environmental factors among twin pairs with autism. Archives of General Psychiatry 68(11): 1095-1102.

Hertz-Picciotto I and Delwiche L（2009） The rise in autism and the role of age at diagnosis. Epidemiology 20（1）: 84-90.

Hillman RE, Kanafani N, Takahashi TN, et al.（2000） Prevalence of autism in Missouri: changing trends and the effect of a comprehensive state autism project. Missouri

Medicine 97 (5): 159–163.

Honberg LE, Kogan MD, Allen D, et al. (2009) Progress in ensuring adequate health insurance for children with special health care needs. Pediatrics 124 (5): 1273–1280.

Honda H, Shimizu Y, Imai M, et al. (2005) Cumulative incidence of childhood autism: a total population study of better accuracy and precision. Developmental Medicine and Child Neurology 47: 10–18.

Kim YS, Leventhal BL, Koh YJ, et al. (2011) Prevalence of autism spectrum disorders in a total population sample. The American Journal of Psychiatry 168 (9): 904–912.

Kogan MD, Blumberg SJ, Schieve LA, et al. (2009) Prevalence of parent-reported diagnosis of autism spectrum disorder among children in the US, 2007. Pediatrics 124 (5): 1395–1403.

Levy D, Ronemus M, Yamrom B, et al. (2011) Rare de novo and transmitted copy-number variation in autistic spectrum disorders. Neuron 70 (5): 886–897.

Lichtenstein P, Carlström E, Råstam M, et al. (2010) The genetics of autism spectrum disorders and related neuropsychiatric disorders in childhood. The American Journal of Psychiatry 167 (11): 1357–1363.

Liu K, Zerubavel N and Bearman P (2010) Social

demographic change and autism. Demography 47(2): 327-343.

Lord C, Risi S, Dilavore PS, et al. (2006) Autism from 2 to 9 yearsof age. Archives of General Psychiatry 63(6): 694-701.

Mandell DS, Wiggins LD, Carpenter LA, et al. (2009) Racial/ethnic disparities in the identification of children with autism spectrum disorders. American Journal of Public Health 99(3): 493-498.

Newschaffer CJ, Croen LA, Daniels J, et al. (2007) The epidemiology of autism spectrum disorders. Annual Review of Public Health 28: 235-258.

Newschaffer CJ, Falb MD and Gurney JG (2005) National autism prevalence trends from United States special education data. Pediatrics 115: 277-282.

Parner E, Schendel D and Thorsen P (2008) Autism prevalence trends over time in Denmark. Archives of Pediatrics & Adolescent Medicine 162(12): 1150-1156.

Posserud MB, Lundervold AJ and Gillberg C (2006) Autistic features in a total population of 7-9-year-old children assessed by the ASSQ (autism spectrum screening questionnaire). Journal of Child Psychology and Psychiatry 47(2): 167-175.

Prior M, Eisenmajer R, Leekam S, et al. (1998) Are there

subgroups with the autistic spectrum? A cluster analysis of a group of children with autism spectrum disorders. Journal of Child Psychology and Psychiatry 39: 893–902.

Thomas P, Zahorodny W, Peng B, et al. (2011) Autism associated with socio-economic status. Autism. 2012 Mar;16 (2): 201–13. Epub 2011 Aug 2.

United States. Bureau of the Census. (1991). American factFinder Retrieved from http://factfinder.census.gov/servlet/Basic FactsServlet (Accessed: October 2011).

Weiss LA (2009) Autism genetics: emerging data from genomewide copy-number and single nucleotide polymorphism scans. Expert Review of Molecular Diagnostics 9: 795–803.

Wing L and Potter D (2002) The epidemiology of autistic spectrum disorders: is the prevalence rising? Mental Retardation and Developmental Disabilities Research Reviews 8 (3): 151–161.

Yeargin-Allsopp M, Rice C, Karapurkar T, et al. (2003) Prevalence of autism in a US metropolitan area. Journal of the American Medical Association 289 (1): 49–55.

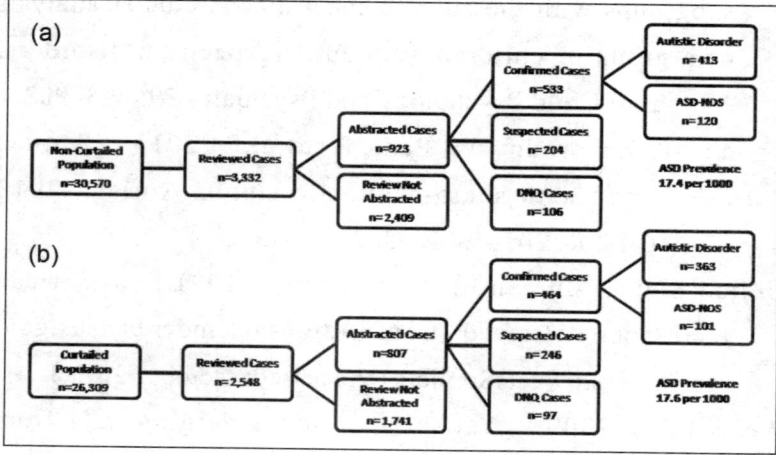

Figure 1. Study diagram. (a) Describes the 2006 study population, ASD was found to be 17.4 per 1000 children and (b) describes the curtailed population in 2006, which is used in comparison to data from SY2002, ASD prevalence was found to be slightly higher than 17.6 per 1000 children.
ASD: autism spectrum disorder; SY: study year.

Further Reading 附录

Table 1. Prevalence of ASD among children aged 8 years, 2002–2006 rate ratio, and percentage of prevalence change—NJAS, 2002 and 2006.

| Category | 2006 population[a] | | 2006 prevalence rate (95% CI)[a] | 2002 population[b] | | 2002 prevalence rate | 2006 population[b] | | 2006 prevalence rate | 2002–2006 rate ratio | | % Change from 2002 to 2006 |
|---|---|---|---|---|---|---|---|---|---|---|---|---|
| | Total no. | Total confirmed no. | | Total No. | Total confirmed no. | | Total no. | Total confirmed no. | | Ratio | 95% CI | |
| Overall | | | | | | | | | | | | |
| Total | 30,570 | 533 | 17.4 (16.0–19.0) | 28936 | 312 | 10.8 | 26,309 | 464 | 17.6 | 1.65** | (1.42–1.90) | 63 |
| Sex | | | | | | | | | | | | |
| Male | 15,739 | 446 | 28.3 (25.8–31.1) | 14953 | 254 | 17.0 | 13,533 | 388 | 28.7 | 1.71** | (1.46–2.00) | 69 |
| Female | 14,831 | 87 | 5.87 (4.75–7.24) | 13983 | 58 | 4.15 | 12,776 | 76 | 5.95 | 1.44* | (1.02–2.02) | 43 |
| Race/ethnicity | | | | | | | | | | | | |
| White, non-Hispanic | 13,599 | 278 | 20.4 (18.2–23.0) | 12247 | 155 | 12.7 | 11,387 | 240 | 21.1 | 1.68** | (1.37–2.06) | 66 |
| Black, non-Hispanic | 7719 | 116 | 15.0 (12.5–18.0) | 7827 | 61 | 7.79 | 6569 | 97 | 14.8 | 1.91** | (1.38–2.63) | 90 |
| Hispanic | 7609 | 112 | 14.7 (12.2–17.7) | 7272 | 72 | 10.0 | 6876 | 103 | 15.1 | 1.51* | (1.12–2.05) | 51 |
| Asian | 1573 | 22 | 14.0 (9.21–21.24) | 1520 | 22 | 14.5 | 1414 | 20 | 14.1 | 1.03 | (0.56–1.88) | 2.9 |
| Race/ethnicity and sex | | | | | | | | | | | | |
| Male | | | | | | | | | | | | |
| White, non-Hispanic | 7011 | 242 | 34.5 (30.4–39.1) | 6267 | 127 | 20.6 | 5855 | 202 | 34.5 | 1.73** | (1.38–2.16) | 70 |
| Black, Non-Hispanic | 3694 | 91 | 23.0 (18.7–28.2) | 4050 | 50 | 12.3 | 3383 | 75 | 22.2 | 1.81** | (1.26–2.60) | 80 |
| Hispanic | 3882 | 91 | 23.4 (19.1–28.8) | 3827 | 57 | 14.9 | 3496 | 83 | 23.7 | 1.61* | (1.14–2.26) | 59 |
| Asian | 837 | 17 | 20.3 (12.6–32.7) | 775 | 18 | 22.7 | 761 | 17 | 21.8 | 0.96 | (0.49–1.88) | 1.3 |
| Female | | | | | | | | | | | | |
| White, non-Hispanic | 6588 | 36 | 5.46 (3.94–7.58) | 5980 | 28 | 4.68 | 5532 | 33 | 6.01 | 1.28 | (0.78–2.13) | 27 |
| Black, Non-Hispanic | 3755 | 25 | 6.66 (4.50–9.85) | 3777 | 11 | 2.91 | 3186 | 21 | 6.59 | 2.72* | (1.09–4.72) | 126 |
| Hispanic | 3727 | 21 | 5.63 (3.67–8.64) | 3445 | 15 | 4.35 | 3380 | 19 | 5.62 | 1.29 | (0.66–2.55) | 29 |
| Asian | 736 | 5 | 6.79 (2.83–16.3) | 745 | 4 | 5.34 | 653 | 3 | 4.57 | 0.86 | (0.19–3.84) | –14 |
| ASD diagnosis/classification | | | | | | | | | | | | |
| ASD diagnosis on record | 30,570 | 367 | 12.01 (10.8–13.3) | 28936 | 193 | 6.67 | 26,309 | 307 | 11.7 | 1.76** | (1.47–2.11) | 75 |
| Special education classification: autism | 30,570 | 227 | 7.43 (6.52–8.46) | 28936 | 130 | 4.49 | 26,309 | 195 | 7.41 | 1.66** | (1.32–2.07) | 65 |
| NJAS—definitions | | | | | | | | | | | | |
| NJAS defined: autism type | 30,570 | 413 | 13.51[c] | 28936 | 227 | 7.84 | 26,309 | 363 | 13.8 | 1.77** | (1.50–2.09) | 76 |
| NJAS defined: ASD-NOS type | 30,570 | 120 | 3.92[c] | 28936 | 85 | 2.94 | 26,309 | 101 | 3.84 | 1.31 | (0.98–1.75) | 31 |
| Regression | 30,570 | 98 | 3.20[c] | 28936 | 67 | 2.31 | 26,309 | 84 | 3.20 | 1.38* | (1.00–1.90) | 38 |

ASD: autism spectrum disorder; NJAS: New Jersey Autism Study; ASD-NOS: autism spectrum disorder–not otherwise specified; CI: confidence interval; SY: study year.
ASD prevalence rate is given per 1000 children aged 8 years old. American Indian Race is not included due to very small number. a Total 8-year-old population for SY2006 noncurtailed. b Total 8-year-old population for SY2002 and SY2006 are curtailed to reflect a common study area between SY2002 and SY2006.
c CIs are not calculated. *p < 0.05, **p < 0.001

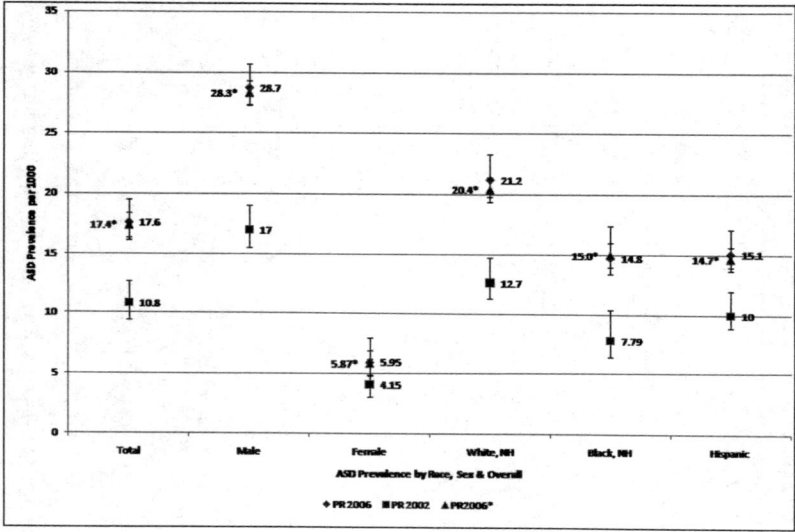

Figure 2. Comparison of ASD prevalence between SY2002 and SY2006.
ASD: autism spectrum disorder; SY: study year

Table 2. Comparison of study methodology and characteristics between SY2002 and SY2006.

| New Jersey Autism Study—characteristics | | | | | | | | |
|---|---|---|---|---|---|---|---|---|
| Category | SY2002 | | | | SY2006 | | | % Change from 2002 to 2006 |
| | Median | SD | Range | N | Median | SD | Range | N | |
| **Data collection** | | | | | | | | |
| Curtailed 8-year-old population | 28,936 | | | | 26,309 | | | | −9 |
| Total reviewed cases in each SY from the total population (n, %) | 2335, 8.1% | | | | 2548, 9.7% | | | | 20 |
| Total abstracted cases from total population (n, %) | 419, 1.4% | | | | 807, 3.1% | | | | 113 |
| Number of confirmed cases in each study year from total abstracted cases | 312, 74.3% | | | | 464, 57% | | | | −22.6 |
| **Study methodology** | | | | | | | | |
| Percentage of children with both educational and health information reviewed | 259, 83.0% | | | | 398, 85.8% | | | | 3.37 |
| Percentage of children receiving autism test | 55, 17.6% | | | | 99, 21.3% | | | | 21.0 confirmed cases only |
| Average number of evaluations per child | 7 | 4.78 | 1–36 | 419 | 7 | 5.04 | 1–41 | 807 | 0 |
| **ASD—age** | | | | | | | | |
| Age of ASD diagnosis noted in child record (months) | 52.50 | 20.53 | 15–101 | 210 | 48.00 | 22.02 | 9–102 | 305 | −8.57 |
| Earliest age of evaluation (months) | 43.50 | 18.84 | 3–105 | 312 | 39.00 | 19.34 | 1–99 | 464 | −10.34 |
| **Developmental concerns** | | | | | | | | |
| Category | SY2002 | | | | SY2006 | | | | % Change from 2002 to 2006 |
| Developmental concerns before age of 3 (n, %) | 279, 89.4% | | | | 416, 89.6% | | | | 0.21 |
| Regression (n, %) | 67, 21.5% | | | | 84, 19.6% | | | | −15.3 |
| IQ ≤ 70 | 76, 24.3% | | | | 108, 23.3% | | | | −4.11 |
| **Special education** | | | | | | | | |
| Autistic classification (n, %) | 133, 42.5% | | | | 206, 44.3% | | | | 4.33 |
| Total confirmed cases receiving special education (n, %) | 306, 98% | | | | 440, 95% | | | | −3 |
| NJ Pk thru 12 receiving special education (%) | 16.1% | | | | 16.6% | | | | 2.6 |
| **New Jersey birth certificate linkage** | | | | | | | | |
| Confirmed cases born in NJ (n, %) | 262, 84% | | | | 379, 82% | | | | −2.4 |

ASD: autism spectrum disorder; SY: study year; SD: standard deviation.
NJ Pk thru 12, refers to school years, pre-Kindergarten thru 12th grade

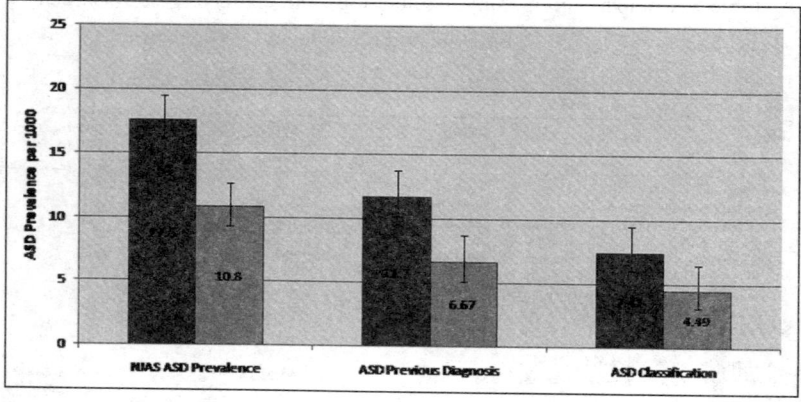

Figure 3. ASD prevalence rate in SY2002 and SY2006 by method of identification. ASD: autism spectrum disorder; SY: study year.

# Prevalence and Characteristics of Autism Spectrum Disorder Among Children Aged 8 Years — Autism and Developmental Disabilities Monitoring Network, 11 Sites, United States, 2012

Deborah L. Christensen, PhD [1]

Jon Baio, EdS [1]

Kim Van Naarden Braun, PhD [1]

Deborah Bilder, MD [2]

Jane Charles, MD [3]

John N. Constantino, MD [4]

Julie Daniels, PhD [5]

Maureen S. Durkin, PhD [6]

Robert T. Fitzgerald, PhD [4]

Margaret Kurzius-Spencer, PhD [7]

Li-Ching Lee, PhD [8]

Sydney Pettygrove, PhD [7]

Cordelia Robinson, PhD [9]

Eldon Schulz, MD [10]

Chris Wells, PhD [11]

Martha S. Wingate, DrPH [12]

Walter Zahorodny, PhD [13]

Marshalyn Yeargin-Allsopp, MD [1]

[1] Division of Congenital and Developmental Disorders, National Center on Birth Defects and Developmental Disabilities, CDC

[2] University of Utah, Salt Lake City

[3] Medical University of South Carolina, Charleston

[4] Washington University in St. Louis, Missouri

[5] University of North Carolina, Chapel Hill

[6] University of Wisconsin–Madison

[7] University of Arizona, Tucson

[8] Johns Hopkins University

[9] University of Colorado at Denver and Health Sciences Center

[10] University of Arkansas for Medical Sciences, Little Rock

[11] Colorado Department of Public Health and Environment, Denver

[12] University of Alabama at Birmingham

[13] Rutgers University–New Jersey Medical School, Newark

## Abstract

Problem/Condition: Autism spectrum disorder (ASD).

Period Covered: 2012.

Description of System: The Autism and Developmental

Further Reading 附录

Disabilities Monitoring (ADDM) Network is an active surveillance system that provides estimates of the prevalence and characteristics of ASD among children aged 8 years whose parents or guardians reside in 11 ADDM Network sites in the United States (Arkansas, Arizona, Colorado, Georgia, Maryland, Missouri, New Jersey, North Carolina, South Carolina, Utah, and Wisconsin). Surveillance to determine ASD case status is conducted in two phases. The first phase consists of screening and abstracting comprehensive evaluations performed by professional service providers in the community. Data sources identified for record review are categorized as either 1) education source type, including developmental evaluations to determine eligibility for special education services or 2) health care source type, including diagnostic and developmental evaluations. The second phase involves the review of all abstracted evaluations by trained clinicians to determine ASD surveillance case status. A child meets the surveillance case definition for ASD if one or more comprehensive evaluations of that child completed by a qualified professional describes behaviors that are consistent with the Diagnostic and Statistical Manual of Mental Disorders, Fourth Edition, Text Revision diagnostic criteria for any of the following conditions: autistic disorder, pervasive developmental disorder–not otherwise specified (including

atypical autism), or Asperger disorder. This report provides ASD prevalence estimates for children aged 8 years living in catchment areas of the ADDM Network sites in 2012, overall and stratified by sex, race/ethnicity, and the type of source records (education and health records versus health records only). In addition, this report describes the proportion of children with ASD with a score consistent with intellectual disability on a standardized intellectual ability test, the age at which the earliest known comprehensive evaluation was performed, the proportion of children with a previous ASD diagnosis, the specific type of ASD diagnosis, and any special education eligibility classification.

Results: For 2012, the combined estimated prevalence of ASD among the 11 ADDM Network sites was 14.6 per 1,000 (one in 68) children aged 8 years. Estimated prevalence was significantly higher among boys aged 8 years (23.6 per 1,000) than among girls aged 8 years (5.3 per 1,000). Estimated ASD prevalence was significantly higher among non-Hispanic white children aged 8 years (15.5 per 1,000) compared with non-Hispanic black children (13.2 per 1,000), and Hispanic (10.1 per 1,000) children aged 8 years. Estimated prevalence varied widely among the 11 ADDM Network sites, ranging from 8.2 per 1,000 children aged 8 years (in the area of the Maryland site where only health care records were reviewed) to 24.6 per 1,000 children aged 8 years (in New Jersey, where both education and health care records were reviewed). Estimated prevalence was higher in surveillance sites where education records and health records were reviewed compared with sites where health records only were reviewed (17.1 per 1,000 and 10.7 per 1,000 children aged 8 years, respectively; p<0.05). Among children identified with ASD by the ADDM Network, 82% had a previous ASD diagnosis or educational classification; this did not vary by sex or between non-Hispanic white and non-Hispanic black children. A lower percentage of Hispanic children (78%) had a previous ASD diagnosis or classification compared with nonHispanic white children (82%) and with non-Hispanic black children (84%). The median age at earliest known comprehensive evaluation was 40 months, and 43% of children had received an earliest known comprehensive evaluation by age 36 months. The percentage of children with an earliest known comprehensive evaluation by age 36 months was similar for boys and girls, but was higher for non-Hispanic white children (45%) compared with non-Hispanic black children (40%) and Hispanic children (39%).

Interpretation: Overall estimated ASD prevalence was 14.6 per 1,000 children aged 8 years in the ADDM Network sites in 2012. The higher estimated prevalence among sites that reviewed both education and health records suggests the

role of special education systems in providing comprehensive evaluations and services to children with developmental disabilities. Disparities by race/ethnicity in estimated ASD prevalence, particularly for Hispanic children, as well as disparities in the age of earliest comprehensive evaluation and presence of a previous ASD diagnosis or classification, suggest that access to treatment and services might be lacking or delayed for some children.

Public Health Action: The ADDM Network will continue to monitor the prevalence and characteristics of ASD among children aged 8 years living in selected sites across the United States. Recommendations from the ADDM Network include enhancing strategies to 1) lower the age of first evaluation of ASD by community providers in accordance with the Healthy People 2020 goal that children with ASD are evaluated by age 36 months and begin receiving community-based support and services by age 48 months; 2) reduce disparities by race/ethnicity in identified ASD prevalence, the age of first comprehensive evaluation, and presence of a previous ASD diagnosis or classification; and 3) assess the effect on ASD prevalence of the revised ASD diagnostic criteria published in the Diagnostic and Statistical Manual of Mental Disorders, Fifth Edition.

Further Reading 附录

## Introduction

Autism spectrum disorder (ASD) is a developmental disability characterized by social and communication impairments and by restricted interests and repetitive behaviors (1). The first studies of the prevalence of autism were published in the 1960s and 1970s, when autism was thought to be a very severe condition, usually accompanied by intellectual disability (2). These studies reported the prevalence to be approximately four to five cases per 10,000 children. Autism was first distinguished as a unique clinical diagnosis by the American Psychiatric Association with the publication in 1980 of the third edition of the Diagnostic and Statistical Manual of Mental Disorders (DSM-III) (3), which provided diagnostic criteria for infantile autism and pervasive developmental disorder. Since that time, autism has become recognized as a spectrum of behavioral characteristics, which results in varying degrees of functional limitations. In 1994, the Diagnostic and Statistical Manual of Mental Disorders, Fourth Edition (DSM-IV) introduced revised diagnostic criteria and five subtypes of autism, including autistic disorder, Asperger disorder, pervasive developmental disorder–not otherwise specified (PDD-NOS), childhood disintegrative disorder, and Rett's disorder (4). The first three subtypes comprise autism spectrum disorder (ASD), whereas the latter two conditions belong to the wider category of pervasive developmental disorders. The fifth edition of DSM, which was published in 2013 (5), redefined ASD as a single disorder, along with other changes in the diagnostic classification of ASD. For this report, the evaluations contained in children's records were conducted no later than 2012, and therefore DSM-IV-TR diagnostic criteria were used in the ASD surveillance case definition to estimate ASD prevalence and characteristics.

Substantial increases in the estimated prevalence of ASD in the United States have been reported since the 1990s. Two studies conducted in the late 1980s that used DSM-III screening and diagnostic criteria for pervasive developmental disorder estimated prevalence as 3.3 cases per 10,000 children aged 3–18 years (6) and 3.6 cases per 10,000 children aged 8–12 years (7). Since then, increases in estimated ASD prevalence have been measured, using data from special education and other administrative records (8–10), national surveys (11–14), and active public health surveillance conducted through CDC's Metropolitan Atlanta Developmental Disabilities Surveillance Program (MADDSP) and its extended surveillance network, the Autism and Developmental Disabilities Monitoring (ADDM) Network. MADDSP first estimated ASD prevalence among children aged 3–10 years in 1996 to be 3.4 per 1,000 children aged 3–10 years (15).

Subsequently, the larger ADDM Network estimated prevalence across multiple U.S. sites every 2 years during 2000–2010. The most recent prevalence estimate from the ADDM Network for children aged 8 years was 14.7 per 1,000 children in 2010（16）, compared with 11.3 in 2008 （17）, 9.0 in 2006 （18）, 6.6 in 2002 （19）, and 6.7 in 2000 （20）.

The American Academy of Pediatrics recommends that pediatric health care providers administer two ASD screenings, at ages 18 and 24 months, using a valid and reliable screening tool （21）. Children whose screening results are concerning should subsequently receive a comprehensive developmental evaluation from a general or developmental pediatrician, child neurologist, child psychiatrist, or child psychologist, which can be obtained privately or through the Part C（ages 0–<3 years）or Part B （ages 3–21 years） programs of the Individuals with Disabilities Education Act （http://idea.ed.gov/explore/home） supported by each state. To support and measure progress in early identification, the Healthy People 2020 initiative includes a goal to increase the percentage of children with ASD who receive their first comprehensive evaluation by age 36 months by 10%, from the baseline of 42.7% in 2006 to the goal of 47.0% in 2020 （22）. ADDM Network ASD surveillance data for children aged 8 years are used to evaluate progress toward this goal.

This report describes estimated ASD prevalence and characteristics among children aged 8 years in the ADDM Network in 2012. This includes 1) total estimated ASD prevalence as well as prevalence by surveillance site, sex, and race/ethnicity and 2) characteristics of children with ASD, including presence of intellectual disability, age at earliest known comprehensive evaluation, presence of a previous ASD diagnosis or educational classification, age at previous ASD diagnosis and diagnosis subtype, and special education eligibility classification. The intended audience for this report includes health care providers, early intervention service providers, therapists, school psychologists, educators, researchers, policymakers, and program administrators seeking to understand and provide for the needs of persons with ASD and their families. These data can be used to help plan for service needs, stimulate research into etiology and risk factors, and initiate and implement policies that promote optimal outcomes in health care and education.

## Methods ADDM Network Sites

The ADDM Network is an active surveillance system that provides estimates of the prevalence and characteristics of ASD among children aged 8 years whose parents or guardians reside within 11 ADDM sites in the United States (selected counties or parts of counties in Arkansas, Arizona, Colorado, Georgia, Maryland, Missouri, New Jersey, North Carolina, South Carolina, Utah, and Wisconsin). The ADDM Network uses multisite, multiple-source surveillance based on a review of behavioral descriptions and ASD diagnoses documented in comprehensive developmental evaluations present in children's health and education records, using a model developed by CDC's MADDSP (15,23). The ADDM Network sites were selected through a competitive process, with preference for a diverse population in terms of race/ethnicity. Each ADDM site functions as a public health authority under the Health Insurance Portability and Accountability Act of 1996 Privacy Rule and meets applicable local Institutional Review Board, privacy, and confidentiality requirements under 45 CFR 46 (24).

### Case Ascertainment

Children eligible for case ascertainment were born in 2004, and their parents or guardians lived in site-specific ADDM Network surveillance catchment areas at some time during 2012. At each site, surveillance data were linked to the state's 2004 birth certificate records to obtain data on race/ethnicity and other demographic characteristics. If a birth certificate match was not made, the child was assumed to have been born

outside the state. No clinical examinations of children were performed by ADDM Network staff.

ADDM Network investigators use a two-phase surveillance approach to ascertain potential ASD cases. The first phase involves screening and abstracting records from multiple data sources in the community, including special education programs and health care providers who evaluate and treat children with developmental disabilities. Agreements to access records are made at the institutional level in the form of contracts, memoranda, or other formal agreements. In the second phase, all abstracted evaluations are compiled and reviewed by clinicians with specialized training in the evaluation and diagnosis of ASD, including physicians, psychologists, and speech/language pathologists. These clinician reviewers follow the ADDM surveillance protocol to determine ASD case status and to maintain reliability.

Data sources identified for record review are categorized as either 1) education source type, including developmental evaluations to determine eligibility for special education services or 2) health care source type, including diagnostic and developmental evaluations. All ADDM Network sites have agreements in place to access records at health care sources. For the 2012 surveillance year, six sites (Arizona, Georgia, New Jersey, North Carolina, South Carolina, and Utah) also reviewed education records in all or most of the surveillance area. In the Maryland site, education records were reviewed in one of the six participating counties, and in the Colorado site, education records were reviewed for some of the public school districts in one of the seven counties in the surveillance area. For these two surveillance sites, only health care source type records were reviewed in the remaining counties. Three sites (Arkansas, Missouri, and Wisconsin) reviewed records only at health care sources.

In the first phase of surveillance, ADDM Network sites identify source records to review on the basis of a child's year of birth and either 1) eligibility classifications in special education or 2) International Classification of Diseases, Ninth Revision, Clinical Modification (ICD-9-CM) billing codes for select childhood disabilities or conditions. Children's records are screened to confirm year of birth and whether the parent or guardian of the child lived in the surveillance area at any

time during the surveillance year. For children meeting age and residency requirements, the source files are screened for specific behavioral or diagnostic descriptions defined by ADDM as triggers for abstraction. These triggers include a documented ASD classification (either a diagnosis of ASD or a special education placement category of ASD) and/or descriptions of behaviors consistent with an ASD diagnosis (e.g., limited or no interaction with other children or prefers objects over persons). If abstraction triggers are found, available information from birth through the current surveillance year is abstracted, including: 1) information on demographic characteristics; 2) other medical conditions; 3) evaluation dates and verbatim descriptions of behaviors consistent with ASD from comprehensive developmental evaluations by community professionals; 4) community professional type and degree (e.g., MD [neurologist, psychiatrist, or developmental pediatrician], PhD [psychologist], or EdS [education specialist]); 5) developmental history, including statements about parental or professional concerns that the child's development was atypical; 6) special education service category; 7) scores from intelligence quotient (IQ), adaptive, and autism diagnostic tests; and 8) evaluation conclusions. The most recent eligibility classification for receiving special education services (e.g., autism or learning disability) is collected from special education records. For all abstracted evaluations, information from multiple sources is combined into one composite summary record for each child.

In the second phase of surveillance, referred to as "clinician review," the abstracted composite evaluation records are deidentified and reviewed systematically by clinicians who have undergone standardized training to determine ASD case status using a coding scheme based on the DSM-IV-TR (1) criteria for ASD. A child meets the surveillance case definition for ASD if behaviors described in the composite record are consistent with the DSM-IV-TR diagnostic criteria for any of the following conditions: autistic disorder, PDD-NOS (including atypical autism), or Asperger disorder. ASD surveillance case criteria were based on DSM-IV-TR because surveillance was conducted using records generated before or during 2012, prior to publication of new diagnostic criteria in the Diagnostic and Statistical Manual of Mental Disorders, Fifth Edition (DSM-5) (5). For the majority of children, one clinician reviews the composite record. If a child meets the surveillance case criteria, but the reviewer is uncertain whether ASD is the most appropriate classification, a second, independent review is done. Following the second review, the two reviewers meet and come to a consensus on the child's case status.

### Descriptive Characteristics

The diagnostic summaries from each evaluation record were abstracted for each child, including age at and subtype of any previous ASD diagnoses. Children were considered to have a previously documented ASD classification if the

child received a DSM-IV-TR diagnosis of autistic disorder, Asperger disorder, PDD-NOS, or ASD-NOS, or if ASD was documented by an ICD-9-CM billing code at any time from birth through the year when the child reached age 8 years, or if the child received special education services under an autism eligibility during the surveillance year. Information was collected on children's functional abilities, including scores on standardized tests of intellectual ability. The most recently recorded scores from tests of a child's intellectual ability were used to categorize the child in the intellectual disability range if the intelligence quotient (IQ) score was ≤ 70, in the borderline range if the score was 71–85, and in the average to above-average range if the score was >85. The child's age at the earliest comprehensive evaluation was documented and is reported as the median age at the earliest comprehensive evaluation in months and as the percentage of children with an earliest known comprehensive evaluation performed by age 36 months. Information also was recorded about the age at which developmental concerns were documented in the records. Analyses of the age at earliest known comprehensive evaluation and the age at which developmental concerns first were documented were restricted to children who were born in the state in which they resided at age 8 years. This restriction was imposed to reduce bias that might have resulted from the unavailability of evaluations performed early in life when the child was residing in a state other than the state in which the ADDM Network site was located.

Quality Assurance

All ADDM Network sites follow the same quality assurance protocol. In the first phase of case ascertainment, screening and abstraction of source records are monitored for accuracy by means of a 10% random sample of records to check the accuracy of data collection as well as the appropriate selection of the record for abstraction. Initial interrater reliability among ASD clinician reviewers was established to a minimum standard of 90% agreement on their decision about whether the child meets the ASD surveillance case definition defined in the ADDM study protocol prior to the beginning of the second phase of case ascertainment. Subsequently, interrater reliability for clinician reviewers is monitored on an ongoing basis using a blinded, random 10% sample of abstracted records that are scored independently by two reviewers. The final interrater agreement for determining surveillance ASD case status（ASD case versus not ASD case）was 90.4% when reliability samples from all ADDM Network sites were combined（K = 0.8）.

## Analytic Methods

The prevalence estimate of ASD among children in the ADDM Network was calculated as the number of children aged 8 years who met the surveillance ASD case definition across the 11 ADDM Network sites in 2012 divided by the number of children aged 8 years residing in the counties comprising the 11 surveillance sites. Population denominators used were obtained from CDC's National Center for Health Statistics (NCHS) vintage 2014 postcensal bridged-race population estimates for 2012 (http://www.cdc.gov/nchs). In the Arizona site, only part of a county was included in the surveillance catchment area. Therefore, the number of children in this county who lived within the surveillance area was estimated in order to obtain the appropriate denominator. This was done by obtaining the third-grade school enrollment counts for the years 2012–2013 for the public school districts included in the surveillance area from the National Center for Education Statistics (https://nces.ed.gov). The number of third-grade students enrolled in the public school districts included in the surveillance area was divided by the number of third-grade students enrolled in all of the public school districts in the county to obtain the proportion of students enrolled in participating school districts. This proportion was then applied to the NCHS vintage 2014 postcensal bridged-race population estimate for each county

Further Reading 附录

in 2012 to obtain the relevant denominator. The bridged-race categories used in this report include non-Hispanic white, non-Hispanic black, Hispanic, American Indian/Alaska Native, and Asian/Pacific Islander. Data from all ADDM sites were pooled to produce combined ASD prevalence estimates. Prevalence estimates were stratified by surveillance site, sex, and race/ethnicity (i.e., non-Hispanic white, non-Hispanic black, and Hispanic). Other race/ethnicity groups were represented by too few children to generate stable estimates of ASD prevalence at all surveillance sites. The race/ethnicity of each child whose records were abstracted was determined from information contained in source records or, if not found in the source records, from birth certificates (when available). Hispanic refers to all children who are of Hispanic ethnicity, regardless of race. Overall prevalence estimates included all children identified with ASD regardless of sex, race/ethnicity, or intellectual ability and therefore were not limited to children with available data on these characteristics.

  Statistical tests were used and confidence interval (CI) estimates were calculated following the assumption that the observed counts of ASD surveillance cases were drawn from an underlying Poisson sampling distribution. Pearson chi-square tests and prevalence ratios (PR) were used to examine the association between ASD prevalence estimates and

characteristics of children with ASD by surveillance site, record source type, sex, and race/ethnicity. Exact tests were used when the number of children was fewer than five. The nonparametric median test was used to determine differences in median age at first evaluation for ASD and earliest known ASD diagnosis by sex and race/ethnicity. Statistical significance was set at $p<0.05$. All analyses were performed by using SAS statistical software（SAS Institute, Cary, North Carolina）.

### Evaluation Methods

Some children who were identified for screening could not be included in the ADDM Network ASD case determination process because some or all of the education and health records could not be found for review. Therefore, an analysis was performed to determine the potential effect of these missing records on ASD prevalence estimates. All children initially identified for screening were first stratified by two factors closely associated with final case status: information source （health source type only, education source type only, or both source types）and the presence or absence of either an autism special education eligibility or an ICD-9-CM code for ASD, collectively forming six strata. The potential number of cases that might have been identified if missing records had been included was estimated by assuming that within each

Further Reading 附录

of these six strata, the proportion of children with ASD in each stratum (with and without missing records) would be similar. Subsequently, the proportion of children meeting the ASD surveillance case definition was applied to the number of children with missing records in the same stratum to estimate the number of missed cases and the corresponding increase in prevalence. Estimates from all six strata were added to produce the total for each site. The analysis of the potential effect of missing records was performed for evaluation purposes, and the prevalence estimates presented in this report do not reflect this adjustment.

### Comparison of Surveillance Sites between 2010 and 2012

For eight sites (Arizona, Colorado, Georgia, Missouri, New Jersey, North Carolina, Utah, and Wisconsin), the geographic area covered and record source type reviewed were the same in 2012 and 2010. Therefore, these eight sites were included in analyses comparing estimated ASD prevalence in 2010 and 2012. For two sites (Arkansas and Maryland), there was a change in geographic area and/or record source type. South Carolina contributed data in 2012 but not in 010. An ADDM Network site located in Alabama conducted ASD surveillance for part of the 2012 surveillance year, but because of the loss of access to health care data sources, data from

Alabama were not complete for the 2012 surveillance year and are not included in this report.

### Results Population Characteristics

The geographic surveillance area for the 11 ADDM Network sites in 2012 included 346,978 children aged 8 years, which comprised 8.5% of the U.S. population of children aged 8 years for that year (Table 1). The population distribution of children by race/ethnicity varied by study site. In the pooled data, the population was 53.3% non-Hispanic white, 21.4% non-Hispanic black, 19.9% Hispanic, 4.8% Asian/Pacific Islander, and 0.6% American Indian/Alaska Native.

### Record Review

A total of 48,304 records for 38,038 children aged 8 years were reviewed from education and health care sources. Among these, the source records of 9,629 (19%) children met the criteria for abstraction and subsequently were reviewed by clinicians. Of these 9,629 children, 5,063 (53%) met the ASDsurveillance case criteria.

### Birth Certificate Linkage

Of the 5,063 children meeting the ASD surveillance case criteria, 3,881 children (77%) were born in the state where

Further Reading 附录

the ADDM Network surveillance site is located, as confirmed by a match to a birth certificate from that state. This percentage ranged from 68% (South Carolina) to 86% (Missouri). The percentage of children who were matched to a birth certificate did not vary by sex or race/ethnicity.

### Overall ASD Prevalence Estimates

Overall estimated ASD prevalence for the 2012 surveillance year was 14.6 per 1,000 (one in 68) children aged 8 years, on the basis of pooled data from 11 ADDM sites (range: 8.2 [Maryland, health records only reviewed] to 24.6 [in New Jersey]) (Table 2). Estimated ASD prevalence was highest in New Jersey (24.6), Maryland (education and health records reviewed, 18.2), Utah (17.3), and North Carolina (16.9). The seven areas (Arizona, Georgia, Maryland [education and health records reviewed], New Jersey, North Carolina, South Carolina, and Utah) with access to both education and health care sources had higher estimated ASD prevalence compared with the five areas (Arkansas, Colorado, Maryland [health records only reviewed], Missouri, and Wisconsin) with limited or no access to education records (17.1 and 10.7 per 1,000 children aged 8 years, respectively; PR: 1.6; 95% CI: 1.5–1.7; p<0.001) (Figure 1).

## Prevalence by Sex and Race/Ethnicity

Across the 11 ADDM Network sites, estimated ASD prevalence among children aged 8 years was 23.6 per 1,000 (one in 42) boys and 5.3 per 1,000 (one in 189) girls; sitespecific ASD estimates for boys ranged from 13.9 per 1,000 (in Maryland [health records only reviewed]) to 39.1 per 1,000 (in New Jersey), and for girls from 2.2 per 1,000 (in Maryland) to 9.3 per 1,000 (in New Jersey) (Table 2). The overall prevalence ratio for boys compared with girls was 4.5 (95% CI: 4.2–4.8; $p<0.001$); site-specific male-to-female prevalence ratios ranged from 4.1 (in Colorado) to 6.3 (in Maryland [health records only reviewed]) and were all statistically significant (Table 2). Estimated prevalence among non-Hispanic white children (15.5 per 1,000) was significantly higher than it was among non-Hispanic black children (13.2 per 1,000; PR: 1.2, 95% CI: 1.1–1.3; $p<0.001$), Asian/Pacific Islander children (11.3 per 1,000; PR: 1.4, 95% CI: 1.2–1.6; $p<0.001$), and Hispanic children (10.1 per 1,000; PR: 1.5, 95% CI: 1.4–1.7; $p<0.001$) (Table 3). Prevalence ratios by sex and race/ethnicity were similar between the areas that reviewed education and health records and the areas that reviewed health records only (Tables 2 and 3).

## Intellectual Ability

Nine ADDM Network areas (Arizona, Arkansas, Colorado, Georgia, Maryland [education and health records review area], New Jersey, North Carolina, South Carolina, and Utah) had data on intellectual ability for ≥ 70% of ASD cases (range: 70% [Arkansas and New Jersey]–92% [in North Carolina]). In these nine areas, 3,390 (80%) of 4,234 children with ASD had data on intellectual ability; for most areas, this percentage did not vary by sex or race/ethnicity, with the exception of Georgia, where the percentage of ASD cases with data on intellectual ability was significantly higher for boys compared with girls (87% and 79%, respectively; $p<0.05$). Among all 3,390 children, 31.6% were classified in the range of intellectual disability (IQ score ≤ 70 or the presence of an examiner's statement of intellectual disability), 24.5% were classified in the borderline range (IQ: 71–85), and 43.9% were classified in the average or above average range (IQ >85 or the presence of an examiner's statement of average or above average intellectual ability) (Figure 2). The percentage of children classified in the intellectual disability range varied widely across the nine areas, ranging from 20% (in Utah) to 50% (in Arkansas). The percentage of ASD cases classified in the intellectual disability range was significantly higher among girls compared with boys in all nine areas combined （37% and 30%, respectively; p<0.01）.

Combining data from all nine sites, the estimated prevalence of ASD with intellectual disability was 4.0 per 1,000 and ranged from 1.8 per 1,000 （in Colorado） to 5.3 per 1,000 （in North Carolina）（Figure 3）. The estimated prevalence of ASD without intellectual disability was 8.7 per 1,000 and ranged from 4.2 per 1,000 （in Arkansas） to 12.2 per 1,000 （in New Jersey）（Figure 3）. There was a greater male-to-female prevalence ratio for ASD without intellectual disability （PR: 5.1; 95% CI: 4.6–5.7; p<0.001） than for ASD with intellectual disability （PR: 3.7; 95% CI: 3.2–4.3; p<0.001）（Figure 4）. The estimated prevalence of ASD with intellectual disability was significantly lower for non-Hispanic white children （3.3 per 1,000） compared with non-Hispanic black children （5.8 per 1,000; PR: 0.6; 95% CI: 0.5–0.7; p<0.001）（Figure 4）.

### Early Developmental Concerns and Earliest Comprehensive Evaluation

Analyses of the presence of early developmental concerns and earliest comprehensive evaluation were restricted to children born in the state where the ADDM Network surveillance site was located in order to reduce bias associated with the inability to review early evaluations for hildren who moved from their state of birth prior to ascertainment by the ADDM Network at age 8 years. Across all ADDM Network sites, 87% of children meeting the ASD surveillance case criteria had documentation of developmental concerns at age $\leq$ 36 months in a health or education record (Table 4). This percentage was similar for areas that reviewed education and health records compared with areas that reviewed health records only (87% and 88%, respectively); the percentage was significantly higher for non-Hispanic black children (91%) and for Hispanic children (89%) compared with non-Hispanic white children (86%; p<0.05). The percentage of children with developmental concerns at age $\leq$ 36 months was significantly higher for children with ASD and intellectual disability compared with children with ASD without intellectual disability (95% and 84%, respectively; p<0.001).

Using combined data from all sites for children meeting the ASD surveillance case criteria and restricting to children born in the state where the ADDM Network surveillance site was located, the earliest known comprehensive evaluation occurred at age $\leq$ 36 months for 43% of children, between 37 and 48 months for 20% of children, and after 48 months for the remaining 38% of children (Table 4). This percentage did not vary between boys and girls (42% and 45%, respectively; p>0.05), but was significantly higher for non-Hispanic white children (45%) compared with nonHispanic black children (40%; p<0.05) and with Hispanic children (39%; p<0.05) (data not shown). Children with ASD and intellectual disability were more likely to have an earliest known comprehensive evaluation by age 36 months compared with children with ASD without intellectual disability (55% and 39%, respectively; p<0.001) (data not shown). The median age at earliest known comprehensive evaluation was 40 months, ranging from 30 months (North Carolina) to 48 months (Arkansas) (data not shown).

### Earliest Known ASD Diagnosis and Diagnosis Category

On the basis of pooled data from all ADDM Network sites, 74% of children identified with ASD had an earliest known DSM-IV-TR ASD diagnosis of autistic disorder (46%), ASD-NOS/PDD-NOS (44%), or Asperger disorder (10%) given by a community provider (Table 5). The median age at the earliest known diagnosis was 50 months overall and was lower for autistic disorder (46 months) compared with ASD-NOS/ PDD-NOS (49 months; p<0.01) and with Asperger disorder (74 months; p<0.001) (Table 5). Within each specific diagnosis subtype, there were no differences in median age at earliest known diagnosis by sex or race/ethnicity (data

Further Reading 附录

not shown).

## Special Education Eligibility

The seven ADDM Network areas that reviewed records at education sources obtained data on the eligibility categories through which children with ASD were served in the public school special education system. Combined data from these seven areas indicate that 74% of children with ASD had special education records; this percentage ranged from 55% (Utah) to 92% (Arizona). Among these children, more than half had a primary special education eligibility classification of autism (range: 53% [in Utah]–70% [in Maryland education and health records review area]) (Table 6). Combining data from all seven areas, the percentage of children with an autism eligibility classification did not vary between boys (61%) and girls (57%; $p>0.05$) or between non-Hispanic white (56%) and Hispanic children (56%; $p>0.05$) but was greater for non-Hispanic black children (65%) compared with non-Hispanic white ($p<0.01$) and Hispanic ($p<0.01$) children (data not shown).

## Previously Documented ASD Classification

Across the 11 ADDM Network sites, 82% of children who met the ASD surveillance case criteria had either a previous diagnosis of ASD or a documented eligibility classification of autism in the special education system, 9% had a suspicion of ASD documented in an evaluation, and the remaining 9% had no mention of ASD in the records (Figure 5). At individual ADDM Network sites, the percentage of children with a previous ASD diagnosis or eligibility classification ranged from 68% (Colorado) to 93% (Missouri) (Figure 5). The percentage of children with a previous ASD diagnosis or eligibility classification was the same for boys and girls (82%) and similar for non-Hispanic white and non-Hispanic black children (82% and 84%, respectively), but was significantly lower for Hispanic children (78%) compared with non-Hispanic white children ($p<0.01$) and non-Hispanic black children ($p<0.001$) (data not shown).

### Comparison of ASD Prevalence Estimates Between 2010 and 2012

For eight sites (Arizona, Colorado, Georgia, Missouri, New Jersey, North Carolina, Utah, and Wisconsin), the geographic areas covered and record source types reviewed were the same for 2010 and 2012. On the basis of combined data from these eight sites in each respective year, estimated ASD prevalence was 15.1 and 15.2 per 1,000 children aged 8 years in 2010 and 2012, respectively ($p>0.05$) (Table 7).

Further Reading 附录

Estimated ASD prevalence for male, female, non-Hispanic white, non-Hispanic black, or Hispanic children did not differ significantly between 2010 and 2012. Five of these eight sites collected data on intellectual ability for ≥ 70% of the children identified with ASD. On the basis of combined data from these five sites in each respective year, estimated ASD prevalence was 17.5 and 17.6 per 1,000 children aged 8 years in 2010 and 2012, respectively （p>0.05） and was similar between 2010 and 2012 for male, female, non-Hispanic white, non-Hispanic black, and Hispanic children （Table 8）. Prevalence estimates were similar for 2010 and 2012 for children with ASD with intellectual disability and for children with ASD without intellectual disability.

Although overall estimated ASD prevalence between 2010 and 2012 was similar across the eight sites that were comparable between these 2 years, the same was not true of all of the individual surveillance sites, three of which had significantly different prevalence estimates in 2012 compared with 2010. Between these two surveillance years, ASD prevalence increased by 16% in Wisconsin and by 12% in New Jersey and decreased by 19% in Missouri.

### Evaluation of the Effect of Missing Records

An evaluation of the effect of missing records suggested

that estimated ASD prevalence might have increased by 0.1% (in Wisconsin) to 3.3% (in Utah) if missing records had been available for review. Across all 11 sites, estimated ASD prevalence might have increased by <1% in four sites Arizona, Colorado, Missouri, and Wisconsin), by 1%–<2% in three sites (Georgia, North Carolina, and New Jersey) and by 2.0%–3.3% in four sites (Arkansas, Maryland, South Carolina, and Utah).

Discussion

Estimated ASD prevalence among children aged 8 years in the ADDM Network in 2012 was 14.6 per 1,000, or one in 68. Estimated prevalence was four and a half times higher among boys than among girls; estimated ASD prevalence was 23.6 per 1,000 boys (one in 42 boys) and 5.3 per 1,000 girls (one in 189 girls). Prevalence estimates varied widely among the 11 ADDM Network sites, ranging from 8.2 per 1,000 children aged 8 years (in the area of the Maryland site where health records only were reviewed) to 24.6 per 1,000 (in New Jersey, where both education and health records were reviewed). The estimated prevalence of ASD with intellectual disability was 4.0 per 1,000 overall and ranged from 1.8 per 1,000 (in Colorado) to 5.3 per 1,000 (in North Carolina). The estimated prevalence of ASD without intellectual disability was 8.7 per 1,000 overall, ranged from 4.2 per 1,000 (in Arkansas) to 12.2 per 1,000 (in New Jersey), and exceeded the estimated prevalence of ASD with intellectual disability in all sites. Across all ADDM Network sites, estimated ASD prevalence was 20% higher among non-Hispanic white compared with non-Hispanic black children, 40% higher among non-Hispanic white compared with Asian/Pacific Islander children, 50% higher among non-Hispanic white compared with Hispanic children, and 30% higher among non-Hispanic black compared with Hispanic children.

The overall prevalence estimate for 2012 was nearly identical to the reported estimate for the ADDM Network in 2010 of 14.7 per 1,000, or one in 68 children aged 8 years. However, because of differences between 2010 and 2012 in the geographic area covered and record source types reviewed for some individual ADDM Network sites, comparing the overall prevalence estimates might be misleading. For this reason, comparisons of ASD prevalence estimates between 2010 and 2012 were restricted to the eight sites for which the geographic surveillance area and record source type reviewed were comparable between the two surveillance years, including five sites with sufficient information on intellectual ability among children with ASD for both years. When results were restricted to these eight sites, combined ASD prevalence estimates were

similar for 2010 and 2012, including in subgroups defined by sex and race/ethnicity. In the five sites with data on intellectual ability, the estimated prevalence of ASD with and without intellectual disability was unchanged in 2012 compared with 2010. This is notable given that the increase in estimated ASD prevalence that has occurred since 2002 has been accompanied by a greater increase in ASD without intellectual disability than ASD with intellectual disability.

Despite the similar findings when the population was restricted to these eight sites for 2010 and 2012 (15.1 and 15.2 per 1,000, respectively), there were significant differences in ASD prevalence estimates between 2010 and 2012 for three of these sites. Significantly increased ASD prevalence estimates were observed in New Jersey (12%) and Wisconsin (16%). In Missouri, estimated ASD prevalence decreased significantly, by 19%, and at the remaining five sites (Arizona, Colorado, Georgia, North Carolina, and Utah), ASD prevalence estimates did not change. The factors underlying the prevalence estimate changes at individual ADDM Network sites are not clear. The two sites with the greatest change from 2010 to 2012 (Missouri and Wisconsin) both reviewed only health source type records for 2010 and 2012. The ability to obtain a comprehensive developmental evaluation through the health care system might be subject to greater local variation compared with evaluations performed through the education system because of changes in the number and availability of providers, changes in insurance coverage policies, or other factors. In addition, changes in record retention associated with migration to electronic health records could limit the availability of historical evaluations at some sources. The wide range of ASD prevalence estimates reported by sites participating in the 2012 ADDM Network coupled with the prevalence estimate increases at some sites suggest the need for caution in interpreting the similarity of overall estimated ASD prevalence between 2010 and 2012. Data from additional surveillance years are needed to understand the trajectory of ASD prevalence.

Population-based estimates of ASD prevalence in the United States also are reported by two CDC surveys. The National Health Interview Study (NHIS) is a nationally representative household survey, and the National Survey of Children's Health (NSCH) is a nationally representative survey of households with children aged 0–17 years in the United States. Both surveys base ASD prevalence estimates on parent or caregiver report of being told by a doctor or other health care provider that the child had ASD. Both NHIS and NSCH ask if the parent/caregiver was ever told that the child has ASD ("ever ASD"); NSCH also includes a follow-up question asking whether the child currently has ASD ("current

ASD") . A previous analysis showed that 13% of parents who reported ever being told that the child had ASD also reported that the child did not currently have ASD; most of these parents attributed the lack of a current ASD diagnosis to new information, suggesting that basing prevalence estimates on ever ASD might overestimate prevalence compared with current ASD (25). For the 2014 NHIS, the prevalence of parent or caregiver-reported ever ASD was 22.4 per 1,000 children aged 3–17 years (26). For the 2011–2012 NSCH, the prevalence of parent or caregiver-reported current ASD was 20 per 1,000 children aged 6–17 years (11). The 2012 ADDM Network overall ASD prevalence estimate of 14.6 per 1,000 is lower than the overall estimates reported in these surveys; however, differences

in the sample population and methodology should be taken into account when comparing results for these three studies. The 2011–2012 NSCH included children aged 6–17 years; when further stratified by age, ASD prevalence was 18.2 per 1,000 children aged 6–9 years and 23.9 per 1,000 children aged 10–13 years. Although the difference in ASD prevalence between these two age groups in the NSCH was not statistically significant, the estimate for children aged 6–9 years (18.2 per 1,000) is closer to the 2012 ADDM Network overall ASD prevalence estimate for children aged 8 years (14.6 per 1,000) and similar to the estimate for the 2012 ADDM Network sites that reviewed education and health care records (17.1 per 1,000). The ASD prevalence estimate from the 2007 NSCH (11.6 per 1,000 children aged 6–17 years) (13) was similar to 2008

ADDM Network prevalence estimate (11.3 per 1,000 children aged 8 years) (17). Taken as a whole, studies using different methodologies and in different populations have reported converging estimates for ASD prevalence in the United States. Future studies by the ADDM Network will incorporate DSM-5 diagnostic criteria, and ongoing ADDM Network surveillance will provide information regarding ASD prevalence trends using DSM-IV-TR and DSM-5 diagnostic criteria.

Consistent with previous years of ADDM Network surveillance (16–20), the overall male-to-female ASD prevalence ratio was 4.5 in 2012 and has remained largely unchanged across recent surveillance years: 4.5 in 2004 (18), 2006 (18), and 2010 (16) and 4.6 in 2008 (17). A similar male-to-female ASD prevalence ratio was found among school-age children in data from the 2010–2011 NSCH (11). Observed differences in estimated ASD prevalence by child characteristics such as sex and race/ethnicity might indicate areas where ASD identification is incomplete and can provide

data to inform policies and efforts to improve identification of ASD among subgroups, particularly female and nonwhite children who have historically had lower identified prevalence compared with male and nonHispanic white children. The higher estimated prevalence among boys might result from sex-specific differences in ASD isk (27,28) or differences in identification of girls with ASD arising from less well-recognized symptom profiles (29), or both. The lower male-to-female prevalence ratio for ASD with intellectual disability (PR: 3.7) compared with ASD without intellectual disability (PR: 5.1) is consistent with data from previous ADDM Network surveillance years. Continued attention should be paid to ensuring that all children with ASD are identified, regardless of functional status.

Results from ADDM Network ASD surveillance in 2012 continue to indicate disparities in estimated ASD prevalence by race/ethnicity. Across all sites, estimated ASD prevalence among non-Hispanic white children was 20% higher compared with non-Hispanic black children, 40% higher compared with Asian/Pacific Islander children, and 50% higher compared with Hispanic children. In addition, a lower percentage of non-Hispanic black and Hispanic children had an earliest comprehensive evaluation by age 36 months compared with non-Hispanic white children. Observed prevalence differences by race/ethnicity might reflect differences in awareness of ASD or access to specialty diagnostic services (30). For the Hispanic population, studies have identified lack of awareness of ASD, stigma associated with disability, lack of access to health care services due to noncitizenship or low income, and language barriers as factors that might reduce the identification of ASD among Hispanic children (31-35). In the 2009-2010 National Survey of Children with Special Health Care Needs (NSCSHCN), estimated ASD prevalence was nearly 50% higher for non-Hispanic white children (15.3 per 1,000) compared with non-Hispanic black children (10.4 per 1,000) and nearly 300% higher for non-Hispanic white children compared with Hispanic children living in households where the primary language was not English (5.2 per 1,000). In contrast, estimated ASD prevalence was similar for nonHispanic white children compared with Hispanic children living in households where the primary language was English (14.3 per 1,000) (32). Language differences could affect the administration and interpretation of developmental screening and monitoring, impede communication of parental concerns about a child's development or a health care provider's recommendation for further evaluation, and limit access to programs and campaigns aimed at increasing awareness of ASD. If lower prevalence in non-Hispanic black and Hispanic children indicates that not all non-Hispanic black and Hispanic children with ASD are being evaluated and/or diagnosed in the community, the children who are not identified might not receive ASD-related services and supports, including school supports to facilitate educational progress. Targeted strategies are needed to increase awareness and identification of ASD in minority communities.

The consistently greater ASD prevalence estimated with data from sites that reviewed education and health source type records underscores the role that public schools play in the equitable provision of comprehensive evaluations to children with developmental concerns. The Individuals with Disabilities Education Act mandates that states and school districts identify, locate, and evaluate all children with disabilities at no cost to the family, so comprehensive evaluations provided through school systems might be more accessible and affordable compared with evaluations performed through the health care system. However, results from these evaluations might not be reported to the health care provider or included in the health care provider records.

Parents and caregivers should be encouraged to share the results of comprehensive evaluations performed through the school system with the child's health care provider to improve continuity of care and ensure that the health care provider can

Further Reading 附录

make recommendations that are based on the child's needs.

The early identification of ASD is a priority of the American Academy of Pediatrics, which recommends universal ASD screening at ages 18 and 24 months, and by the U.S. Department of Health and Human Services through the Healthy People 2020 goal of a 10% increase in the percentage of children with ASD who receive their first evaluation by age 36 months (22). ADDM Network data are used to measure the goal that 47% of children with ASD have a first evaluation by age 36 months; the baseline percentage for this goal is 42.7%, as measured by ADDM Network data in 2006. Lowering the age at first evaluation is important because when impairments are identified through a comprehensive evaluation, referrals for specific services can be made, often without a formal diagnosis. On the basis of evidence linking early treatment to improved outcomes (36–39), it is important that children with developmental concerns be evaluated and referred to services as soon as possible. In 2010, the percentage of children aged 8 years with ASD residing the ADDM catchment area with an earliest known comprehensive evaluation by age 36 months was 43.8% (16), and the 2012 percentage was similar at 42.8%. Although several years remain before determination of whether the goal was achieved, the lack of progress from the baseline measured in 2006 through 2012 is disappointing. Of note, the age cohort represented here was born in 2004 and therefore the findings regarding the percentage of children with an earliest known evaluation by age 36 months reflect practices during 2004–2007. Continued surveillance is necessary to monitor progress towards the Healthy People 2020 goal, particularly in light of the 2006 AAP screening recommendations, and to identify factors associated with later age at first evaluation so that strategies to improve early referral and evaluation can be developed. ADDM Network surveillance of ASD prevalence and characteristics among children aged 4 years, which began in 2010, can help to provide more timely data on early identification of children with ASD (40).

The availability of records containing developmental evaluations conducted to determine eligibility for special education services as well as those conducted through the health care system in response to concerns about a child's development forms the basis for the public health surveillance of ASD conducted by the ADDM Network. By screening existing records then applying a consistent methodology by trained and research-reliable clinician reviewers to determine case status, the ADDM Network is able to conduct population-based surveillance of ASD in a large and diverse population. This methodology was validated, compared with direct examination of children, and the methods were found to result in a prevalence estimate that is likely conservative (41).

Limitations

The findings in this report are subject to at least seven limitations. First, data were limited to the information available in the source records. The amount and quality of the data define the potential to determine whether a child meets the ASD surveillance case definition and the extent to which the characteristics of the identified population can be described. In particular, data on intellectual ability were not available for all children, and the distribution of intellectual ability among the children with these data might not be generalizable to all children with ASD. Second, the types of source records varied across sites, and the inability to review education records at some sites might have led to an underestimate of ASD prevalence in those sites. Third, education records generally were not available for children attending private school or being home-schooled. Fourth, the surveillance areas were selected through a competitive process and were not selected to be representative of children aged 8 years in the United States or the state where the surveillance site was located. Fifth, county-level population counts for children by sex and race/ethnicity are not available by single year of age in nondecennial census years. Population estimates published by the National Center for Health Statistics are used instead. There is evidence that the error in population estimates for the intervening years between decennial census counts increases with increasing years beyond the decennial census (in this case, 2010) (42). Sixth, the analysis of age at first comprehensive evaluation was restricted to children for whom linkage was made to birth certificates for the state where the ADDM Network site was located in an attempt to reduce bias resulting from the unavailability of early evaluations for children who moved after birth. However, a child might have moved out and back into this state between birth and ascertainment, so this restriction might not have completely eliminated this potential source of bias. Finally, race and ethnicity were defined broadly for this surveillance population, and results for a specific race or ethnic group might not be representative of results for all children in these groups. In addition, it was not possible to distinguish Hispanic children living in households in which the primary language was English from those with a different primary language.

### Future Study Directions

In 2013, revised diagnostic criteria for ASD were published by the American Psychiatric Association in the DSM-5 (5). Beginning with the 2014 surveillance year, the ADDM Network will be able to estimate ASD case status on the basis of both DSM-5 and DSM-IV-TR. This evaluation is possible because of the data collection methods employed since the inception of the ADDM Network, including the abstraction of specific behaviors documented in children's records. This unique component of ADDM Network ASD surveillance will enable the ADDM Network investigators to evaluate the change in estimated ASD prevalence that might arise from the change in diagnostic criteria. Previous analyses have suggested that fewer children will meet the behavioral criteria of DSM-5 compared with DSM-IV-TR (43). However, DSM-5 criteria include a provision that children with a well-established diagnosis of one of the three autism spectrum disorder subtypes under DSM-IV-TR criteria are considered to have ASD under DSM-5 criteria. Therefore, at least for the initial years following the publication of DSM-5, ASD prevalence estimates that are based on DSM-5 criteria should include the children with a DSM-IV-TR-based diagnosis in order to accurately represent the number of children who are being treated and served for ASD by community providers. Because the surveillance methodology of the ADDM Network also includes collection of information on ASD diagnoses by community providers, future estimates of the prevalence of ASD under DSM-5 will be able to include children who meet DSM-5 criteria by virtue of a past DSM-IV-

TR diagnosis as well as those meeting the DSM-5 behavioral criteria.

## Conclusion

Approximately one in 68 children aged 8 years living in sites participating in the ADDM Network surveillance areas met the ASD case criteria for the 2012 surveillance year. Although the overall prevalence estimate is unchanged from surveillance year 2010, prevalence ranged widely across the ADDM Network and prevalence increases were reported at two sites, suggesting that it is premature to conclude that the rising prevalence of ASD observed during the first decade of the 21st century might be slowing. Ongoing surveillance of ASD prevalence through the ADDM Network is likely to provide the most accurate means to monitor trends in ASD prevalence over time, including those that are related to changes in the diagnostic criteria for ASD. ASD surveillance informs providers, particularly public schools, of upcoming service needs, and provides feedback on progress made toward early identification goals. The ADDM Network will continue to track age at first comprehensive evaluation to monitor progress toward the Healthy People 2020 goal of increasing the percentage of children with ASD who receive a first evaluation by age 36 months. Estimated ASD prevalence was substantially lower among Hispanic and non-Hispanic black children compared with non-Hispanic white children. In addition, non-Hispanic black and Hispanic children were less likely to have a first evaluation by age 36 months and Hispanic children were less likely to have a previous ASD diagnosis or classification. This finding suggests that a number of nonwhite children with ASD are not being identified and evaluated, and for those children who are evaluated, a later age at the first comprehensive evaluation likely delays initiation of services for these children. No intervention has been shown to reduce the prevalence of ASD; however, early treatment might maximize the ability of children to function and participate in their community. Initiation of school-based services prior to formal school entry might help to facilitate optimal educational progress. Continued efforts should be made to promote early identification of all children with ASD so that interventions can be initiated at the youngest age possible.

### Acknowledgments

Data collection was coordinated at each site by ADDM Network project coordinators: Eric Lott, University of Alabama at Birmingham; Kristen Clancy Mancilla, University of Arizona, Tucson; Allison Hudson, University of Arkansas for Medical Sciences, Little Rock; Kelly Kast, MSPH, Colorado

Department of Public Health and Environment, Denver; Kwinettaion Jolly, MS, Research

Triangle Institute, Atlanta, Georgia; Anita Washington, MPH, Ann Ussery-Hall, MPH, Lisa Barritt, Gal Frenkel, MPH, Division of Birth Defects and Developmental Disabilities, National Center on Birth Defects and Developmental Disabilities, CDC; Ann Chang, Rebecca Harrington, PhD, Johns Hopkins University, Baltimore, Maryland; Rob Fitzgerald, PhD, Washington University, St. Louis, Missouri; Josephine Shenouda, MS, Rutgers University–New Jersey Medical School, Newark; Paula Bell, University of North Carolina, Chapel Hill; Andrea Boan, PhD, Walter Jenner, MS, Medical University of South Carolina; Colin Kingsbury, MS, Amanda Bakian, PhD, Amy Henderson, University of Utah, Salt Lake City; Pamela Imm, MS, University of Wisconsin–Madison. Additional assistance was provided by Russell Kirby, PhD, University of South Florida, Tampa; Heather Clayton, PhD, Alyson Goodman, MD, Lisa Wiggins, PhD, Division of Congenital and Developmental Disorders, National Center on Birth Defects and Developmental Disabilities, CDC; project staff including data abstractors, clinician reviewers, epidemiologists, and data management/programming support. Ongoing ADDM Network support was provided by Victoria Wright, Tineka Yowe-Conley, National Center on Birth Defects

Further Reading 附录

and Developmental Disabilities, CDC.

References

1. American Psychiatric Association. Diagnostic and statistical manual of mental disorders. 4th ed. Text revision. Washington, DC: American Psychiatric Association; 2000.
2. Gillberg C, Wing L. Autism: not an extremely rare disorder. Acta Psychiatr Scand 1999;99:399–406. http://dx.doi.org/10.1111/j.1600-0447.1999.tb00984.x
3. American Psychiatric Association. Diagnostic and statistical manual of mental disorders. 3rd ed. Washington, DC: American Psychiatric Association; 1980.
4. American Psychiatric Association. Diagnostic and statistical manual of mental disorders. 4th ed. Washington, DC: American Psychiatric Association; 1994.
5. American Psychiatric Association. Diagnostic and statistical manual of mental disorders. 5th ed. Arlington, VA: American Psychiatric Association; 2013.
6. Burd L, Fisher W, Kerbeshian J. A prevalence study of pervasive developmental disorders in North Dakota. J Am Acad Child Adolesc Psychiatry 1987;26:700–3. http://dx.doi.org/10.1097/00004583-198709000-00014
7. Ritvo ER, Freeman BJ, Pingree C, et al. The UCLA-University of Utah epidemiologic survey of autism:

prevalence. Am J Psychiatry 1989;146:194–9. http://dx.doi.org/10.1176/ajp.146.2.194

8. Croen LA, Grether JK, Hoogstrate J, Selvin S. The changing prevalence of autism in California. J Autism Dev Disord 2002;32:207–15. http:// dx.doi.org/10.1023/A:1015453830880

9. Newschaffer CJ, Falb MD, Gurney JG. National autism prevalence trends from United States special education data. Pediatrics 2005;115:e277–82. http://dx.doi.org/10.1542/peds.2004-1958

10. California Department of Developmental Services. Autistic spectrum disorders: changes in the California caseload, an update: 1999 through 2002. Sacramento, CA: California Health and Human Services Agency, Department of Developmental Services; 2003.

11. Blumberg SJ, Bramlett MD, Kogan MD, Schieve LA, Jones JR, Lu MC. Changes in prevalence of parent-reported autism spectrum disorder in school-aged U.S. children: 2007 to 2011–2012. Natl Health Stat Report 2013;65:1–11.

12. Boyle CA, Boulet S, Schieve LA, et al. Trends in the prevalence of developmental disabilities in US children, 1997–2008. Pediatrics 2011;127:1034–42. http://dx.doi.org/10.1542/peds.2010-2989

13. Kogan MD, Blumberg SJ, Schieve LA, et al. Prevalence

of parentreported diagnosis of autism spectrum disorder among children in the US, 2007. Pediatrics 2009;124:1395–403. http://dx.doi.org/10.1542/ peds.2009-1522

14. Schieve LA, Rice C, Yeargin-Allsopp M, et al. Parent-reported prevalence of autism spectrum disorders in US-born children: an assessment of changes within birth cohorts from the 2003 to the 2007 National Survey of Children's Health. Matern Child Health J 2012;16（Suppl 1）:S151–7. http://dx.doi.org/10.1007/s10995-012-1004-0

15. Yeargin-Allsopp M, Rice C, Karapurkar T, Doernberg N, Boyle C, Murphy C. Prevalence of autism in a US metropolitan area. JAMA 2003;289:49–55. http://dx.doi.org/10.1001/jama.289.1.49 16. Autism and Developmental Disabilities Monitoring Network Surveillance Year 2010 Principal Investigators. Prevalence of autism spectrum disorder among children aged 8 years—Autism and Developmental Disabilities Monitoring Network, 11 sites, United States, 2010. MMWR Surveill Summ 2014;63（No. SS-2）.

17. Autism and Developmental Disabilities Monitoring Network Surveillance Year 2008 Principal Investigators. Prevalence of autism spectrum disorders—Autism and Developmental Disabilities Monitoring Network, 14 sites, United States, 2008. MMWR Surveill Summ 2012;61（No.

SS-3）:1-19.
18. Autism and Developmental Disabilities Monitoring Network Surveillance Year 2006 Principal Investigators. Prevalence of autism spectrum disorders—Autism and Developmental Disabilities Monitoring Network, United States, 2006. MMWR Surveill Summ 2009;58（No. SS-10）:1-20.
19. Autism and Developmental Disabilities Monitoring Network Surveillance Year 2002 Principal Investigators. Prevalence of autism spectrum disorders—Autism and Developmental Disabilities Monitoring Network, 14 sites, United States, 2002. MMWR Surveill Summ 2007;56（No. SS-1）:12-28.
20. Autism and Developmental Disabilities Monitoring Network Surveillance Year 2000 Principal Investigators. Prevalence of autism spectrum disorders—Autism and Developmental Disabilities Monitoring Network, six sites, United States, 2000. MMWR Surveill Summ 2007;56（No. SS-1）:1-11.
21. Johnson CP, Myers SM; American Academy of Pediatrics Council on Children with Disabilities. Identification and evaluation of children with autism spectrum disorders. Pediatrics 2007;120:1183-215. http:// dx.doi.org/10.1542/peds.2007-2361

22. US Department of Health and Human Services. Healthy people 2020. Washington, DC: US Department of Health and Human Services; 2010. http://www.healthypeople.gov
23. Yeargin-Allsopp M, Murphy CC, Oakley GP, Sikes RK. A multiplesource method for studying the prevalence of developmental disabilities in children: the Metropolitan Atlanta Developmental Disabilities Study. Pediatrics 1992;89:624-30.
24. US Department of Health and Human Services. Code of Federal Regulations. Title 45. Public Welfare CFR 46. Washington, DC: US Department of Health and Human Services; 2010. http://www.hhs.gov/ ohrp/humansubjects/ guidance/45cfr46.html
25. Blumberg SJ, Zablotsky B, Avila RM, Colpe LJ, Pringle BA, Kogan MD. Diagnosis lost: differences between children who had and who currently have an autism spectrum disorder diagnosis. Autism 2015:1362361315607724.
26. Zablotsky B, Black LI, Maenner MJ, Schieve LA, Blumberg SJ. Estimated prevalence of autism and other developmental disabilities following questionnaire changes in the 2014 National Health Interview Study. Natl Health Stat Report 2015;87:1-20.
27. Lai MC, Lombardo MV, Suckling J, et al.; MRC AIMS Consortium. Biological sex affects the neurobiology

of autism. Brain 2013;136:2799-815. http://dx.doi.org/10.1093/brain/awt216

28. Werling DM, Geschwind DH. Understanding sex bias in autism spectrum disorder. Proc Natl Acad Sci U S A 2013;110:4868-9. http://dx.doi.org/10.1073/pnas.1301602110

29. Andersson GW, Gillberg C, Miniscalco C. Pre-school children with suspected autism spectrum disorders: do girls and boys have the same profiles? Res Dev Disabil 2013;34:413-22. http://dx.doi.org/10.1016/j.ridd.2012.08.025

30. Jarquin VG, Wiggins LD, Schieve LA, Van Naarden-Braun K. Racial disparities in community identification of autism spectrum disorders over time; Metropolitan Atlanta, Georgia, 2000-2006. J Dev Behav Pediatr 2011;32:179-87. http://dx.doi.org/10.1097/DBP.0b013e31820b4260

31. Flores G, Abreu M, Tomany-Korman SC. Why are Latinos the most uninsured racial/ethnic group of US children? A community-based study of risk factors for and consequences of being an uninsured Latino child. Pediatrics 2006;118:e730-40. http://dx.doi.org/10.1542/peds.2005-2599

32. Jo H, Schieve LA, Rice CE, et al. Age at autism spectrum disorder (ASD) diagnosis by race, ethnicity, and primary

household language among children with special health care needs, United States, 2009–2010. Matern Child Health J 2015;19:1687–97. http://dx.doi.org/10.1007/ s10995-015-1683-4

33. Zuckerman KE, Mattox K, Donelan K, Batbayar O, Baghaee A, Bethell C. Pediatrician identification of Latino children at risk for autism spectrum disorder. Pediatrics 2013;132:445–53. http://dx.doi. org/10.1542/peds.2013-0383

34. Zuckerman KE, Sinche B, Cobian M, et al. Conceptualization of autism in the Latino community and its relationship with early diagnosis. J Dev Behav Pediatr 2014;35:522–32. http://dx.doi.org/10.1097/ DBP.0000000000000091

35. Zuckerman KE, Sinche B, Mejia A, Cobian M, Becker T, Nicolaidis C. Latino parents' perspectives on barriers to autism diagnosis. Acad Pediatr 2014;14:301–8. http:// dx.doi.org/10.1016/j.acap.2013.12.004 36. Dawson G, Rogers S, Munson J, et al. Randomized, controlled trial of an intervention for toddlers with autism: the Early Start Denver Model. Pediatrics 2010;125:e17–23. http://dx.doi. org/10.1542/peds.2009-0958

37. Eapen V, Crnčec R, Walter A. Clinical outcomes of an early intervention program for preschool children with Autism

Spectrum Disorder in a community group setting. BMC Pediatr 2013;13:3. http://dx.doi. org/10.1186/1471-2431-13-3

38. Reichow B, Barton EE, Boyd BA, Hume K. Early intensive behavioral intervention (EIBI) for young children with autism spectrum disorders (ASD). Cochrane Database Syst Rev 2012;10:CD009260.

39. Rogers SJ, Estes A, Lord C, et al. Effects of a brief Early Start Denver model (ESDM)-based parent intervention on toddlers at risk for autism spectrum disorders: a randomized controlled trial. J Am Acad Child Adolesc Psychiatry 2012;51:1052–65. http://dx.doi.org/10.1016/j.jaac.2012.08.003

40. Christensen DL, Bilder DA, Zahorodny W, et al. Prevalence and characteristics of autism spectrum disorder among 4-year-old children in the Autism and Developmental Disabilities Monitoring Network. J Dev Behav Pediatr 2016;37:1–8. http://dx.doi.org/10.1097/DBP.0000000000000235

41. Nonkin Avchen R, Wiggins LD, Devine O, et al. Evaluation of a recordsreview surveillance system used to determine the prevalence of autism spectrum disorders. J Autism Dev Disord 2011;41:227–36. http:// dx.doi.org/10.1007/s10803-010-1050-7

42. Lazarus C, Autry A, Baio J, Avchen RN, Van Naarden Braun K. Impact of postcensal versus intercensal population estimates on prevalence owf selected developmental disabilities—metropolitan Atlanta, Georgia, 1991–1996. Am J Ment Retard 2007;112:462–6. http://dx.doi. org/10.1352/0895-8017（2007）112[462:IOPVIP] 2.0.CO;2

43. Maenner MJ, Rice CE, Arneson CL, et al. Potential impact of DSM-5 criteria on autism spectrum disorder prevalence estimates. JAMA Psychiatry 2014;71:292–300. http://dx.doi.org/10.1001/ jamapsychiatry.2013.3893

TABLE 1. Number* and percentage of children aged 8 years, by race/ethnicity and site — Autism and Developmental Disabilities Monitoring Network, 11 sites, United States, 2012

| Site | Site institution | Surveillance area | Total No. | White, non-Hispanic No. | (%) | Black, non-Hispanic No. | (%) | Hispanic No. | (%) | API, non-Hispanic No. | (%) | AI/AN, non-Hispanic No. | (%) |
|---|---|---|---|---|---|---|---|---|---|---|---|---|---|
| Arizona | University of Arizona | Part of 1 county in metropolitan Phoenix | 32,615 | 15,525 | (47.6) | 1,856 | (5.7) | 13,180 | (40.4) | 1,276 | (3.9) | 778 | (2.4) |
| Arkansas | University of Arkansas for Medical Sciences | 16 counties in Arkansas | 14,153 | 9,083 | (64.2) | 3,739 | (26.4) | 1,025 | (7.2) | 226 | (1.6) | 80 | (0.6) |
| Colorado | Colorado Department of Public Health and Environment | 7 counties including metropolitan Denver | 40,538 | 22,370 | (55.2) | 2,469 | (6.1) | 13,448 | (33.2) | 2,029 | (5.0) | 222 | (0.5) |
| Georgia | CDC | 5 counties including metropolitan Atlanta | 49,720 | 16,451 | (33.1) | 20,556 | (41.3) | 9,019 | (18.1) | 3,588 | (7.2) | 106 | (0.2) |
| Maryland† | Johns Hopkins University | 1 county in suburban Baltimore | 9,577 | 5,019 | (52.4) | 3,171 | (33.1) | 656 | (6.9) | 696 | (7.3) | 35 | (0.4) |
| Maryland§ | Johns Hopkins University | 5 counties in suburban Baltimore | 18,154 | 12,293 | (67.7) | 3,042 | (16.8) | 1,384 | (7.6) | 1,383 | (7.6) | 52 | (0.3) |
| Missouri | Washington University–St. Louis | 5 counties including metropolitan St. Louis | 25,870 | 17,211 | (66.5) | 6,516 | (25.2) | 1,109 | (4.3) | 970 | (3.7) | 64 | (0.2) |
| New Jersey | Rutgers University–New Jersey Medical School | 4 counties including metropolitan Newark | 32,581 | 13,829 | (42.4) | 7,100 | (21.8) | 9,787 | (30.0) | 1,781 | (5.5) | 84 | (0.3) |
| North Carolina | University of North Carolina–Chapel Hill | 11 counties in central North Carolina | 38,913 | 20,789 | (53.4) | 9,544 | (24.5) | 6,517 | (16.7) | 1,906 | (4.9) | 157 | (0.4) |
| South Carolina | Medical University of South Carolina | 23 counties in coastal and Pee Dee regions | 24,356 | 12,485 | (51.3) | 9,404 | (38.6) | 1,964 | (8.1) | 387 | (1.6) | 116 | (0.5) |
| Utah | University of Utah | 3 counties in northern Utah | 24,945 | 18,217 | (73.0) | 568 | (2.3) | 4,851 | (19.4) | 1,151 | (4.6) | 158 | (0.6) |
| Wisconsin | University of Wisconsin–Madison | 10 counties in southeastern Wisconsin | 35,556 | 21,758 | (61.2) | 6,342 | (17.8) | 5,915 | (16.6) | 1,392 | (3.9) | 149 | (0.4) |
| Total | | | 346,978 | 185,030 | (53.3) | 74,307 | (21.4) | 68,885 | (19.9) | 16,785 | (4.8) | 2,001 | (0.6) |

Abbreviations: AI/AN = American Indian/Alaska Native; API = Asian/Pacific Islander.
* Total numbers of children aged 8 years in each surveillance area were obtained from CDC's July 1, 2012 bridged-race population estimates.
† Education and health records review area.
§ Health records only review area.

Further Reading 附录

TABLE 2. Estimated prevalence* of autism spectrum disorder among 1,000 children aged 8 years, by sex — Autism and Developmental Disabilities Monitoring Network, 11 sites, United States, 2012

| Site | Total | Total no. with ASD | Total[†] Prevalence (95% CI) | Sex Male Prevalence (95% CI) | Female Prevalence (95% CI) | Male-to-female prevalence ratio[†] |
|---|---|---|---|---|---|---|
| Arizona | 32,615 | 494 | 15.2 (13.9–16.5) | 24.2 (22.0–26.7) | 5.7 (4.7–7.0) | 4.2 (3.4–5.3) |
| Arkansas | 14,153 | 170 | 12.0 (10.3–14.0) | 19.2 (16.3–22.7) | 4.6 (3.2–6.5) | 4.2 (2.9–6.2) |
| Colorado | 40,538 | 436 | 10.8 (9.8–11.8) | 17.1 (15.4–19.0) | 4.2 (3.4–5.2) | 4.1 (3.2–5.2) |
| Georgia | 49,720 | 771 | 15.5 (14.4–16.6) | 25.6 (23.7–27.6) | 5.2 (4.3–6.1) | 4.9 (4.1–6.0) |
| Maryland[§] | 9,577 | 174 | 18.2 (15.7–21.1) | 29.4 (25.0–34.6) | 6.2 (4.3–9.0) | 4.7 (3.2–7.0) |
| Maryland[¶] | 18,154 | 148 | 8.2 (6.9–9.6) | 13.9 (11.7–16.5) | 2.2 (1.4–3.5) | 6.3 (3.9–10.0) |
| Missouri | 25,870 | 297 | 11.5 (10.2–12.9) | 18.9 (16.7–21.4) | 3.8 (2.8–5.0) | 5.0 (3.7–6.8) |
| New Jersey | 32,581 | 800 | 24.6 (22.9–26.3) | 39.1 (36.2–42.2) | 9.3 (7.9–10.9) | 4.2 (3.5–5.0) |
| North Carolina | 38,913 | 656 | 16.9 (15.6, 18.2) | 27.5 (25.3, 29.9) | 6.0 (5.0, 7.2) | 4.6 (3.8–5.6) |
| South Carolina | 24,356 | 302 | 12.4 (11.1–13.9) | 19.9 (17.6–22.5) | 4.6 (3.5–6.0) | 4.3 (3.2–5.8) |
| Utah | 24,945 | 431 | 17.3 (15.7–19.0) | 27.7 (24.9–30.7) | 6.4 (5.1–8.0) | 4.3 (3.4–5.5) |
| Wisconsin | 35,556 | 384 | 10.8 (9.8–11.9) | 17.2 (15.4–19.2) | 4.1 (3.2–5.2) | 4.2 (3.2–5.4) |
| Total | 346,978 | 5,063 | 14.6 (14.2–15.0) | 23.6 (22.9–24.3) | 5.3 (4.9, 5.6) | 4.5 (4.2–4.8) |

Abbreviations: ASD = autism spectrum disorder; CI = confidence interval; E+H = education plus health.
* Per 1,000 children aged 8 years.
[†] All sites identified significantly higher prevalence among males compared with females (Pearson chi-square, p<0.01).
[§] Education and health records review area.
[¶] Health records only review area.

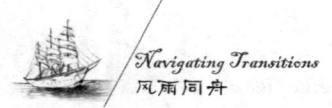

TABLE 3. Estimated prevalence* of autism spectrum disorder among 1,000 children aged 8 years, by race/ethnicity — Autism and Developmental Disabilities Monitoring Network, 11 sites, United States, 2012

| Site | Race/Ethnicity | | | | Prevalence ratio | | |
|---|---|---|---|---|---|---|---|
| | White, non-Hispanic Prevalence (95% CI) | Black, non-Hispanic Prevalence (95% CI) | Hispanic Prevalence (95% CI) | API, non-Hispanic Prevalence (95% CI) | White-to-black | White-to-Hispanic | Black-to-Hispanic |
| Arizona | 16.9 (15.0–19.1) | 19.4 (14.0–26.9) | 11.3 (9.6–13.3) | 13.3 (8.3–21.4) | 0.9 | 1.5† | 1.7† |
| Arkansas | 12.8 (10.4–15.3) | 9.9 (7.2–13.7) | —§ | — | 1.3 | — | — |
| Colorado | 12.2 (10.9–13.8) | 10.5 (7.2–15.1) | 6.5 (5.2–8.0) | 8.4 (5.2–13.5) | 1.2 | 1.9† | 1.6† |
| Georgia | 17.6 (15.6–19.7) | 13.4 (11.9–15.1) | 11.5 (9.5–14.0) | 13.4 (10.1–17.8) | 1.3† | 1.5† | 1.2 |
| Maryland¶ | 18.5 (15.1–22.7) | 18.6 (14.4–24.0) | 12.2 (6.1–24.4) | 10.1 (4.8, 21.1) | 1.0 | 1.5 | 1.5 |
| Maryland** | 8.6 (7.1–10.4) | 6.9 (4.5–10.6) | 5.8 (2.9–11.6) | — | 1.2 | 1.5 | 1.2 |
| Missouri | 12.0 (10.5–13.8) | 9.0 (7.0–11.7) | 8.1 (4.2–15.6) | — | 1.3 | 1.5† | 1.1 |
| New Jersey | 26.6 (24.0–29.5) | 23.7 (20.3–27.5) | 17.6 (15.1–20.4) | 21.9 (16.0–30.0) | 1.1 | 1.5† | 1.3† |
| North Carolina | 18.9 (17.1, 20.8) | 15.5 (13.2, 18.2) | 9.1 (7.0, 11.7) | 18.4 (13.2, 25.6) | 1.2† | 2.1† | 1.7† |
| South Carolina | 12.7 (10.8–14.8) | 10.6 (8.7–12.9) | 6.6 (3.8–11.4) | — | 1.2 | 1.9† | 1.6 |
| Utah | 17.7 (15.8–19.7) | 12.3 (5.9–25.8) | 13.2 (10.3–16.9) | 5.2 (2.3–11.6) | 1.4 | 1.3† | 0.9 |
| Wisconsin | 12.0 (10.6–13.5) | 5.8 (4.2–8.0) | 7.4 (5.5–10.0) | 3.6 (1.5–8.6) | 2.1† | 1.6† | 0.8 |
| Total | 15.5 (14.9–16.1) | 13.2 (12.4–14.0) | 10.1 (9.4–10.9) | 11.3 (9.8, 13.0) | 1.2† | 1.5† | 1.3† |

Abbreviations: API = Asian/Pacific Islander; ASD = autism spectrum disorder; CI = confidence interval; E+H = education plus health.
* Per 1,000 children aged 8 years.
† Prevalence ratio significant at p<0.05.
§ Prevalence not calculated when n<5.
¶ Education and health records review area.
** Health records only review area.

# Further Reading 附录

TABLE 4. Number and percentage of children aged 8 years* identified with autism spectrum disorder who received a comprehensive evaluation by a qualified professional at age ≤36 months, 37–48 months, or >48 months, and those with a mention of a developmental concern by age 36 months — Autism and Developmental Disabilities Monitoring Network, 11 sites, United States, 2012

| Site | Earliest age when child received a comprehensive evaluation | | | Mention of a developmental concern by age 36 months |
|---|---|---|---|---|
| | ≤36 mos | 37–48 mos | >48 mos | |
| | No. (%) | No. (%) | No. (%) | No. (%) |
| Arizona | 149 (39.2) | 70 (18.4) | 161 (42.4) | 341 (89.7) |
| Arkansas | 33 (24.2) | 38 (27.9) | 65 (47.8) | 119 (87.5) |
| Colorado | 131 (40.6) | 60 (18.6) | 132 (40.9) | 278 (86.1) |
| Georgia | 222 (41.1) | 113 (20.9) | 205 (38.0) | 473 (87.6) |
| Maryland[†] | 83 (55.0) | 27 (17.9) | 41 (27.2) | 143 (94.7) |
| Maryland[§] | 34 (31.2) | 22 (20.2) | 53 (48.6) | 101 (92.7) |
| Missouri | 103 (40.6) | 34 (13.4) | 117 (46.1) | 210 (82.7) |
| New Jersey | 277 (42.9) | 137 (21.1) | 233 (36.0) | 527 (81.5) |
| North Carolina | 288 (59.8) | 71 (14.7) | 123 (25.5) | 444 (92.1) |
| South Carolina | 79 (38.5) | 52 (25.4) | 74 (36.1) | 189 (92.2) |
| Utah | 119 (37.5) | 66 (20.8) | 132 (41.6) | 258 (81.4) |
| Wisconsin | 133 (41.8) | 63 (19.8) | 122 (38.4) | 286 (89.9) |
| Total | 1,662 (42.8) | 756 (19.5) | 1,463 (37.7) | 3,386 (87.2) |

* Includes 3,881 children identified with autism spectrum disorder who were linked to an in-state birth certificate.
† Education and health records review area.
§ Health records only review area.

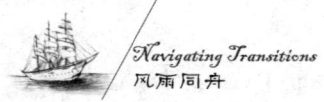

TABLE 5. Median age of earliest known autism spectrum disorder diagnosis and number and proportion within each diagnostic subtype — Autism and Developmental Disabilities Monitoring Network, 11 sites, United States, 2012

| | ASD subtype | | | | | | |
|---|---|---|---|---|---|---|---|
| | Autistic disorder | | ASD-NOS/PDD-NOS | | Asperger disorder | | Any ASD subtype | |
| Site | Median age (mos) | No. (%) | Median age (mos) | No. (%) | Median age (mos) | No. (%) | Median age (mos) | No. (%) |
| Arizona | 50.0 | 254 (74.5) | 64.0 | 72 (21.1) | 77.0 | 15 (4.4) | 55.0 | 341 (69.0) |
| Arkansas | 53.0 | 97 (72.9) | 60.0 | 20 (15.0) | 77.5 | 16 (12.0) | 60.0 | 133 (78.2) |
| Colorado | 48.0 | 184 (66.2) | 59.0 | 55 (19.8) | 80.0 | 39 (14.0) | 55.0 | 278 (63.8) |
| Georgia | 47.5 | 262 (48.0) | 51.0 | 231 (42.3) | 71.0 | 53 (9.7) | 51.0 | 546 (70.8) |
| Maryland* | 41.0 | 56 (40.6) | 48.0 | 79 (57.2) | 44.0 | 3 (2.2) | 45.5 | 138 (79.3) |
| Maryland† | 46.5 | 44 (33.5) | 44.5 | 72 (58.1) | 44.0 | 8 (6.4) | 48.0 | 124 (83.8) |
| Missouri | 50.0 | 67 (26.1) | 51.0 | 145 (56.4) | 78.0 | 45 (17.5) | 58.0 | 257 (86.5) |
| New Jersey | 44.5 | 192 (29.7) | 43.0 | 378 (58.4) | 74.0 | 77 (11.9) | 47.0 | 647 (80.9) |
| North Carolina | 37.0 | 207 (53.6) | 55.5 | 156 (40.4) | 72.0 | 23 (6.0) | 48.0 | 386 (58.8) |
| South Carolina | 45.0 | 143 (65.0) | 58.0 | 70 (31.8) | 74.0 | 7 (3.2) | 48.0 | 220 (72.8) |
| Utah | 45.0 | 114 (31.7) | 48.0 | 178 (49.4) | 63.5 | 68 (18.9) | 50.0 | 360 (83.5) |
| Wisconsin | 45.5 | 106 (34.8) | 49.0 | 173 (56.7) | 74.0 | 26 (8.5) | 50.0 | 305 (79.4) |
| Total | 46.0 | 1,726 (46.2) | 49.0 | 1,629 (43.6) | 74.0 | 380 (10.2) | 50.0 | 3,735 (73.8) |

Abbreviations: ASD-NOS = autism spectrum disorder–not otherwise specified; PDD-NOS = pervasive developmental disorder–not otherwise specified.
* Education and health records review area.
† Health records only review area.

# Further Reading 附录

TABLE 6. Number and percentage of children aged 8 years identified with autism spectrum disorder with available special education records, by primary special education eligibility category* — Autism and Developmental Disabilities Monitoring Network, seven sites, United States, 2012

| Primary special education eligibility category | Arizona | Georgia | Maryland† | New Jersey | North Carolina | South Carolina | Utah |
|---|---|---|---|---|---|---|---|
| Autism (%) | 61.4 | 58.1 | 70.2 | 56.2 | 69.0 | 61.0 | 53.4 |
| Emotional disturbance (%) | 4.6 | 1.1 | 1.6 | 0.7 | 1.4 | 0 | 1.7 |
| Specific learning disability (%) | 6.8 | 3.1 | 8.1 | 4.6 | 7.9 | 4.9 | 8.5 |
| Speech or language impairment (%) | 6.8 | 1.6 | 0 | 10.3 | 2.8 | 2.7 | 18.6 |
| Hearing or visual impairment (%) | 0 | 0.6 | 0 | 0.3 | 0 | 0 | 0 |
| Health or physical disability (%) | 4.4 | 3.7 | 12.1 | 19.1 | 10.4 | 5.4 | 10.6 |
| Multiple disabilities (%) | 2.0 | 0 | 4.0 | 6.4 | 0.8 | 0 | 0 |
| Intellectual disability (%) | 8.2 | 2.6 | 3.2 | 1.0 | 3.8 | 3.6 | 4.2 |
| Developmental delay/preschool (%) | 5.7 | 29.2 | 0.8 | 0.4 | 3.8 | 20.2 | 3.0 |
| Other (%) | 0 | 0 | 0 | 0.9 | 0.2 | 2.2 | 0 |
| Total no. of ASD cases | 494 | 771 | 174 | 800 | 656 | 302 | 431 |
| Total no. (%) of ASD cases with special education records | 454 (91.9) | 621 (80.5) | 124 (71.3) | 698 (87.3) | 507 (77.3) | 223 (73.8) | 236 (54.8) |

Abbreviation: ASD = autism spectrum disorder.
* Some state-specific categories were recoded or combined to match current US Department of Education categories.
† Education and health records review area.

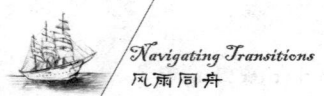

TABLE 7. Comparison of autism spectrum disorder prevalence among sites with comparable surveillance area in 2010 and 2012, by record source type, sex, and race/ethnicity, Autism and Developmental Disabilities Monitoring Network, eight sites, United States

| Characteristic | 2010 Prevalence (95% CI) | 2012 Prevalence (95% CI) | 2012-to-2010 prevalence ratio (95% CI) |
|---|---|---|---|
| **Record source** | | | |
| E+H areas* | 17.5 (16.9–18.2) | 17.6 (17.0–18.3) | 1.01 (0.96–1.06) |
| HO areas[†] | 10.8 (10.1–11.4) | 11.0 (10.4–1.6) | 1.02 (0.94–1.11) |
| E+H-to-HO prevalence ratio | 1.6 (1.5–1.7) | 1.6 (1.5–1.7) | —[§] |
| **Site** | | | |
| Arizona | 15.7 (14.4–17.1) | 15.2 (13.9–16.5) | 0.97 (0.85–1.10) |
| Colorado | 9.9 (9.0–10.9) | 10.8 (9.8–19.0) | 1.09 (0.95–1.25) |
| Georgia | 15.5 (14.3–16.8) | 15.5 (14.4–16.6) | 1.00 (0.90–1.10) |
| Missouri | 14.2 (12.8–15.7) | 11.5 (10.2–12.9) | 0.81 (0.70–0.95) |
| New Jersey | 21.9 (20.4–23.6) | 24.6 (22.9–26.3) | 1.12 (1.01–1.24) |
| North Carolina | 17.3 (16.1–18.7) | 16.9 (15.6–18.2) | 0.97 (0.90–1.08) |
| Utah | 18.6 (16.9–20.4) | 17.3 (15.7–19.0) | 0.93 (0.81–1.06) |
| Wisconsin | 9.3 (8.3–10.3) | 10.8 (9.8–11.9) | 1.16 (1.01–1.35) |
| **Sex** | | | |
| Male | 24.4 (23.6–25.2) | 24.5 (23.7–25.4) | 1.02 (0.96–1.05) |
| Female | 5.4 (5.0–5.8) | 5.5 (5.1–5.9) | 1.02 (0.92–2.13) |
| Male-to-female prevalence ratio | 4.5 (4.2–5.0) | 4.4 (4.1–4.8) | — |
| **Race/Ethnicity** | | | |
| White, non-Hispanic | 16.2 (15.5–16.8) | 16.3 (15.7–17.0) | 1.02 (0.96–1.07) |
| Black, non-Hispanic | 12.9 (12.0–13.9) | 13.9 (12.9–14.9) | 1.07 (0.97–1.19) |
| Hispanic | 11.2 (10.4–12.1) | 10.4 (9.6, 11.2) | 0.93 (0.83–1.03) |
| White-to-black prevalence ratio | 1.3 (1.2–1.4) | 1.2 (1.1–1.3) | — |
| White-to-Hispanic prevalence ratio | 1.4 (1.3–1.6) | 1.6 (1.4–1.7) | — |
| Black-to-Hispanic prevalence ratio | 1.2 (1.0–1.3) | 1.3 (1.2–1.5) | — |
| **Total** | 15.1 (14.6–15.5) | 15.2 (14.7–15.6) | 1.01 (0.97–1.05) |

Abbreviations: CI = confidence interval; E+H = education and health records; HO = health records only review.
* Sites reviewing education and health records: Arizona, Georgia, New Jersey, North Carolina, and Utah.
[†] Sites reviewing health records only: Colorado, Missouri, and Wisconsin.
[§] Ratios of prevalence ratios were not calculated.

TABLE 8. Comparison of autism spectrum disorder prevalence among sites with comparable surveillance areas, by sex, race/ethnicity, and most recent score on intelligence quotient test, Autism and Developmental Disabilities Monitoring Network, five sites,* United States, 2010 and 2012

| Characteristic | 2010 Prevalence (95% CI) | 2012 Prevalence (95% CI) | Prevalence ratio 2012 to 2010 (95% CI) |
|---|---|---|---|
| **Sex** | | | |
| Male | 28.5 (27.4–29.6) | 28.5 (27.4–29.6) | 1.00 (0.95–1.06) |
| Female | 6.2 (5.7–6.8) | 6.3 (5.8–6.9) | 1.02 (0.91–1.15) |
| Male-to-female prevalence ratio | 4.6 (4.2–5.0) | 4.5 (4.1–4.9) | —† |
| **Race/Ethnicity** | | | |
| White, non-Hispanic | 19.4 (18.5–20.4) | 19.3 (18.4–20.3) | 1.00 (0.93–1.07) |
| Black, non-Hispanic | 15.2 (14.0–16.4) | 16.2 (15.0–17.5) | 1.06 (0.95–1.19) |
| Hispanic | 13.5 (12.4–14.6) | 12.1 (11.1–13.2) | 0.90 (0.80–1.01) |
| White-to-black prevalence ratio | 1.3 (1.2–1.4) | 1.2 (1.1–1.3) | — |
| White-to-Hispanic prevalence ratio | 1.4 (1.3–1.6) | 1.6 (1.5–1.8) | — |
| Black-to-Hispanic prevalence ratio | 1.1 (1.0–1.3) | 1.4 (1.2–1.5) | — |
| **IQ** | | | |
| ≤70 | 4.6 (4.3–4.9) | 4.3 (4.0–4.7) | 0.94 (0.86–1.04) |
| >70 | 10.6 (10.1–11.1) | 10.0 (9.6–10.5) | 0.95 (0.89–1.01) |
| Unknown | 2.4 (2.1–2.6) | 3.3 (3.0–3.5) | 1.39 (1.22–1.57) |
| >70-to-≤70 prevalence ratio | 2.3 (2.1–2.5) | 2.3 (2.1–2.5) | — |
| **Total** | 17.5 (16.9–18.2) | 17.6 (17.0–18.3) | 1.01 (0.96–1.06) |

Abbreviations: CI = confidence interval; IQ = intelligence quotient.
* Arizona, Georgia, New Jersey, North Carolina, and Utah.
† Ratios of prevalence ratios were not calculated.

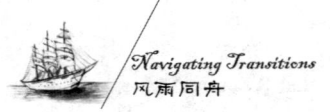

FIGURE 1. Estimated prevalence* of autism spectrum disorder among children aged 8 years — Autism and Developmental Disabilities Monitoring Network, 11 sites, United States, 2012

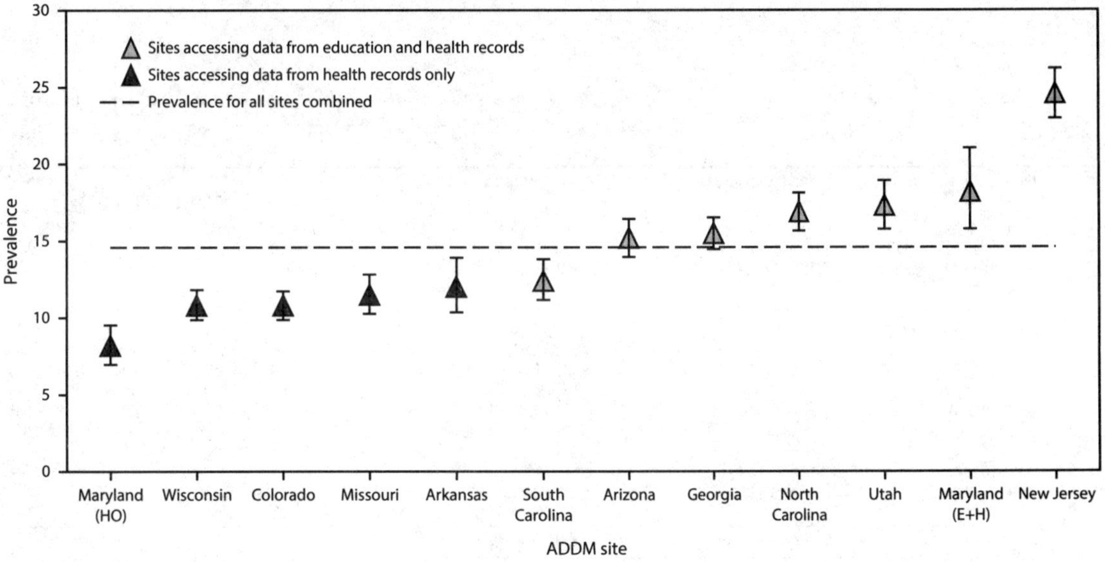

Abbreviations: ADDM = Autism and Developmental Disabilities Monitoring Network; E+H = education and health records; HO = health records only.
* Cases per 1,000 children aged 8 years. Bars represent 95% confidence intervals.

Further Reading 附录

FIGURE 2. Scores of most recent intelligence quotient tests for children identified with autism spectrum disorder for whom test data were available — Autism and Developmental Disabilities Monitoring Network, nine sites,* United States, 2012

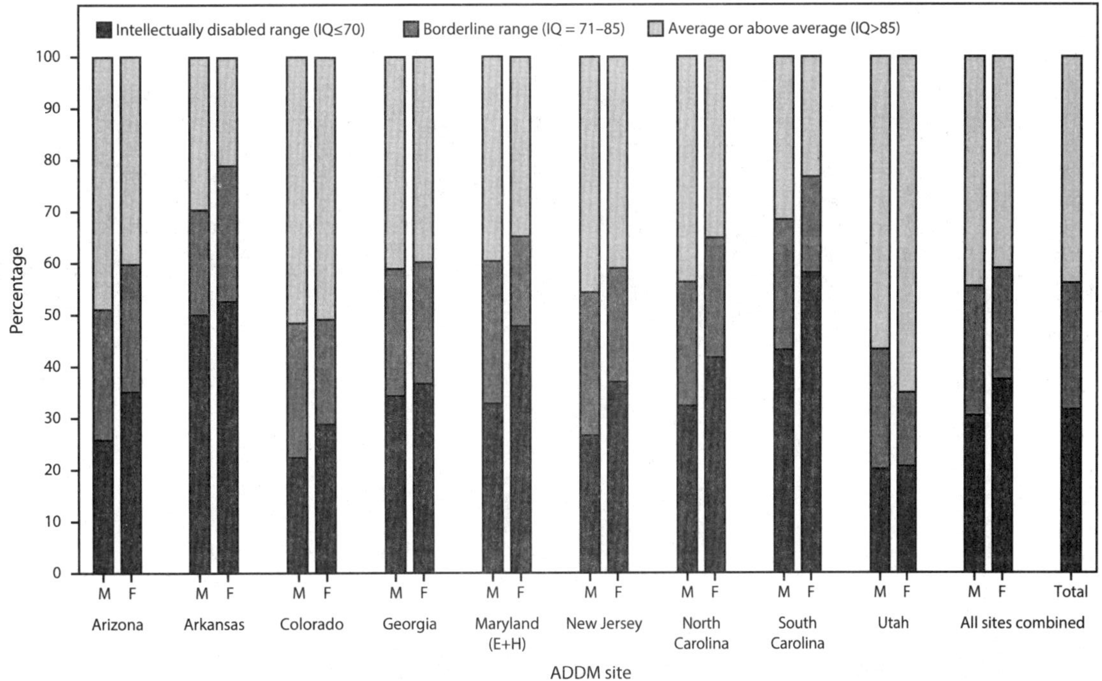

Abbreviations: ADDM = Autism and Developmental Disabilities Monitoring Network; ASD = autism spectrum disorder; E+H = education and health records; IQ = intelligence quotient.
* Includes sites having information on intellectual ability available for ≥70% of children who met the ASD case definition (N = 3,390).

FIGURE 3. Estimated prevalence* of autism spectrum disorder among children aged 8 years, by most recent intelligence quotient score and by site — Autism and Developmental Disabilities Monitoring Network, nine sites, † United States, 2012

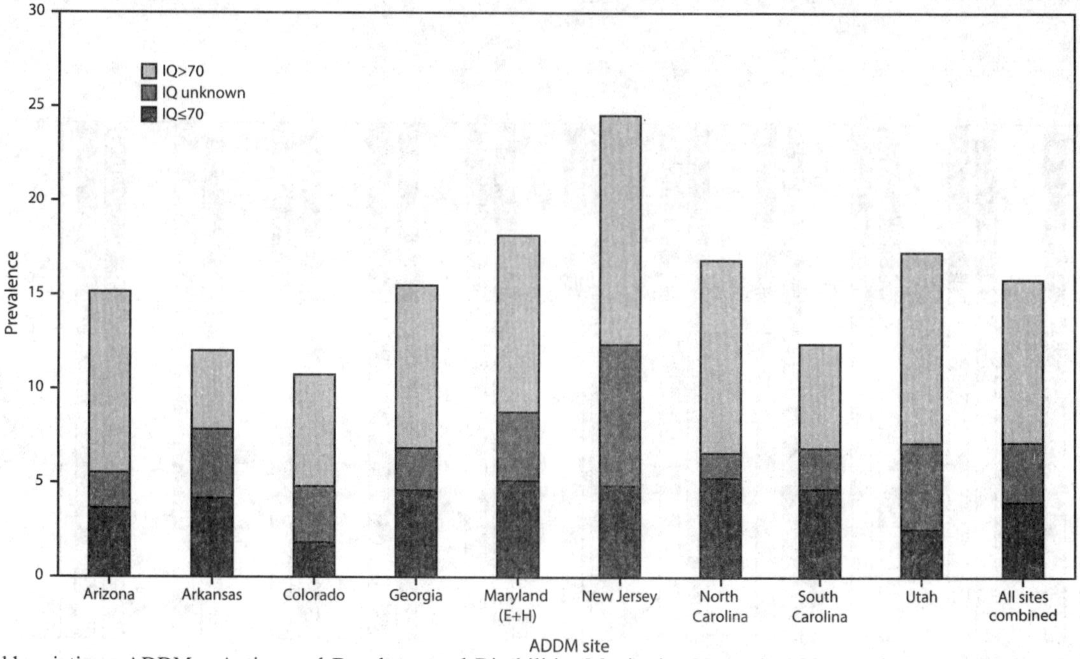

Abbreviations: ADDM = Autism and Developmental Disabilities Monitoring Network; ASD = autism spectrum disorder; E+H = education and health records; IQ = intelligence quotient.
* Cases per 1,000 children aged 8 years.
† Includes sites having information on intellectual ability available for ≥70% of children who met the ASD case definition (N = 3,390). Maryland source type is education and health records.

Further Reading 附录

FIGURE 4. Estimated prevalence* of autism spectrum disorder among children aged 8 years, by most recent intelligence quotient score, by sex and race/ethnicity — Autism and Developmental Disabilities Monitoring Network, nine sites, † United States, 2012

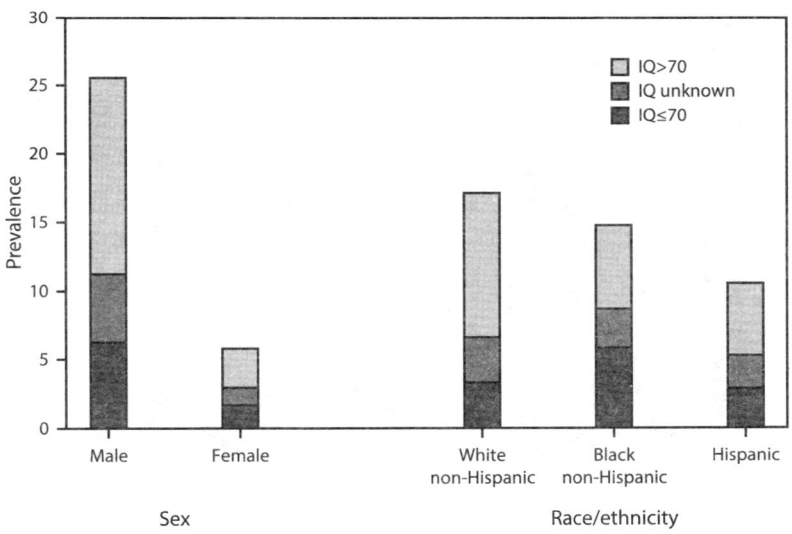

Abbreviations: ASD = autism spectrum disorder; IQ = intelligence quotient.
* Cases per 1,000 children aged 8 years.
† Includes nine sites (Arizona, Arkansas, Colorado, Georgia, Maryland [education and health records],
New Jersey, North Carolina, South Carolina, and Utah) having information on intellectual ability
available for ≥70% of children who met the ASD case definition (N = 3,390).

FIGURE 5. Percentage of children with autism spectrum disorder at age 8 years who had previous autism spectrum disorder classification on record, suspicion of the disorder noted, or no mention of the disorder, by site — Autism and Developmental Disabilities Monitoring Network, 11 sites, United States, 2012

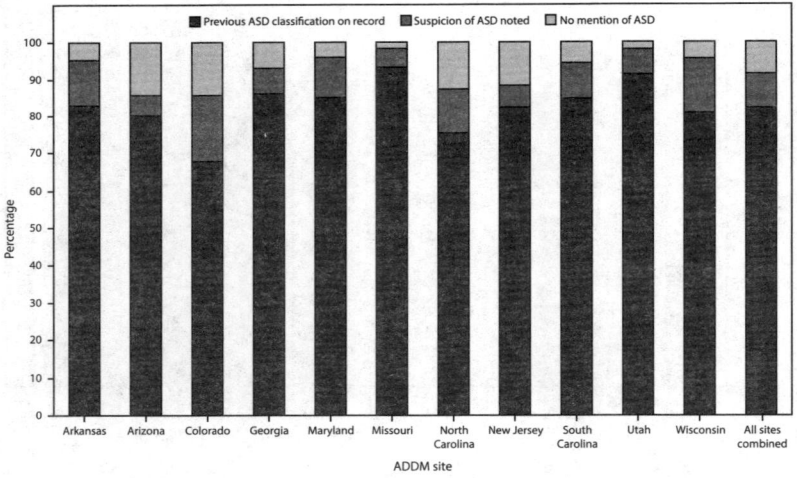

Abbreviations: ADDM = Autism and Developmental Disabilities Monitoring Network; ASD = autism spectrum disorder.

Further Reading 附录

The Morbidity and Mortality Weekly Report (MMWR) Series is prepared by the Centers for Disease Control and Prevention (CDC) and is available free of charge in electronic format. To receive an electronic copy each week, visit MMWR's free subscription page at http://www.cdc.gov/mmwr/mmwrsubscribe.html. Paper copy subscriptions are available through the Superintendent of Documents, U.S. Government Printing Office, Washington, DC 20402; telephone 202-512-1800.

Readers who have difficulty accessing this PDF file may access the HTML file at http://www.cdc.gov/mmwr/volumes/65/ss/ss6503a1.htm?s_cid=ss6503a1_w. Address all inquiries about the MMWR Series, including material to be considered for publication, to Executive Editor, MMWR Series, Mailstop E-90, CDC, 1600 Clifton Rd., N.E., Atlanta, GA 30329-4027 or to mmwrq@cdc.gov.

All material in the MMWR Series is in the public domain and may be used and reprinted without permission; citation as to source, however, is appreciated.

Use of trade names and commercial sources is for identification only and does not imply endorsement by the U.S. Department of Health and Human Services.

References to non-CDC sites on the Internet are provided as a service to MMWR readers and do not constitute or imply endorsement of these organizations or their programs by CDC or the U.S. Department of Health and Human Services. CDC is not responsible for the content of these sites. URL addresses listed in MMWR were current as of the date of publication.